JOHN ASHBERY

COLUMBIA INTRODUCTIONS TO

TWENTIETH-CENTURY

AMERICAN POETRY

JOHN UNTERECKER, GENERAL EDITOR

1. Larry Rivers. "Pyrography" (Fully Painted). Acrylic on canvas, 76 x 58 inches. Courtesy Robert Miller Gallery. (Photo: eeva-inkeri)

JOHN ASHBERY

AN INTRODUCTION
TO THE POETRY

DAVID SHAPIRO

COLUMBIA UNIVERSITY PRESS

NEW YORK

1979

OTHER BOOKS BY DAVID SHAPIRO

January
Poems from Deal
A Man Holding an Acoustic Panel
The Page-Turner
An Anthology of New York Poets
  (coedited with Ron Padgett)
Lateness

Library of Congress Cataloging in Publication Data

Shapiro, David, 1947–
  John Ashbery, an introduction to the poetry.

  (Columbia introductions to twentieth-century American
poetry)
  Bibliography: p.
  Includes index.
  1. Ashbery, John—Criticism and interpretation.
I. Title.   II. Series.
PS3501.S475Z85   811'.5'4   79-4420
ISBN 0-231-04090-3

Columbia University Press
New York—Guildford, Surrey

COLUMBIA INTRODUCTIONS TO TWENTIETH-CENTURY AMERICAN POETRY

To Architecture and To My Architect
Lindsay

Reality is a cliché from which we escape by metaphor. It is only *au pays de la métaphore qu'on est poète.* —Wallace Stevens

Heard melodies are sweet, but those unheard
Are sweeter. —John Keats

Contents

Foreword

The poetry of John Ashbery seems "difficult," I think, only because we normally ask of literature vast simplifications. "Don't," we are always saying to literature, "don't, whatever you are, be as complex as life, as liberty, or as the pursuit of happiness!"

We want literature to be a little difficult, of course, but only a little. A "fruitful ambiguity" flatters us because we have no problem distinguishing paired pears from pared apples, even in a tureen of strawberry jello. And though allegory seems heavy-handed, we enjoy a sophisticated chase through any symbolist jungle. We like always to outsmart the detective, recognizing far sooner than he does that the man in the aquamarine beret is not only not the axe murderer who wore two left shoes but almost certainly the missing husband of the disturbingly un-communicative but beautiful Tasmanian heiress with whom each and every one of us has fallen desperately in love.

Literature normally flatters and reassures us. It shows us what we all want to see: a pattern, no matter how faint, superimposed on chaos. But when the pattern wavers, vanishes, reemerges briefly in the form of a nervous mirage, and then once and for all dissolves into universal jumble, we are likely to become uneasy and possibly cantankerous. "This is difficult stuff," we find ourselves remarking, meaning by *difficult* either *outrageous* or *representational* or both.

The writer who presents normal human experience in something like its everyday complexity really is outrageous. He offends us by not making rational the incomprehensible or, at best, confusing overlaps of routine existence. Instead, he diagrams such stuff as shifting personality, "I" trying to adjust constantly to all the personalities that are busy adjusting to "me." Or he notices how easily anyone projects—frequently with disasterous consequences—his "I" into every "you" in sight, and sometimes fatally fails to do so.

Such a writer, representing the real world of the mind, finds meandering thought his true vocation. What goes on in, say, the assembled heads of an audience during a poetry reading —even one by John Ashbery—would look, if mapped, something like neighboring three-dimensional termite nests. Not just dreamers, daydreamers, and the senile find listening difficult; all of us, most of the time, play peek-a-boo with the stuff that comes in at the ear. We respond to what we hear, all right, but as well to the secondary stimuli that bombard us through eye, nose, mouth, and rubbing skin. For literally everything starts us thinking. We listen to the world most obliquely, tuning in and tuning out, dancing a sort of intellectual buck-and-wing as "private" thoughts commingle quite irrationally with the flow of public phrases that endlessly spill from a jabbering world.

What I am arguing, of course, is that Ashbery's "difficulty" is more imaginary than real. Ashbery presents, often in meticulously representational detail, a normal man's way of apprehending—though not of voicing—reality. In doing so, he is drastically unconventional, since the normal man devotes a great deal of time and energy to disguising the way his mind works. What comes out of the normal man's mouth or type-writer barely resembles the wanderings of his hit-or-miss mind: the ill-heard sentences, the details of his own observation that he can't help notice (the flick of an eyelid, the shadow of a smile), all of the colors, smells, and textures that intrude on him and that, perhaps heroically, he pummels into submission whenever he attempts to "communicate." We are all hard-working citizens of this kind, much of the time either oblivious to the ways in which our heads work or so disturbed by those ways as to pretend we have no heads at all.

Like Gertrude Stein, James Joyce, and others who have at-tempted to ensnare the psychic processes we so carefully sup-press, Ashbery focuses hard on the way the mind deals with the random stuff that drifts into it. But much more recklessly than Stein or Joyce, he offers us not the thoughts of a "persona"—an Alice B. Toklas, for instance, or a Stephen Dedalus—but the abruptly bare phrases that float through his own mind. Or at least he does his best to give us the illusion that those phrases are what he presents, phrases not just obscure but for almost everybody else in the world totally baffling. By drawing on pri-vate materials, he forces us to have the strange experience of roaming through someone else's head. "The landscape looks familiar," we are likely to think as we read through a non-sequeturing Ashbery poem, "but the hands are the hands of Esau."

Once in a while, he lets us glimpse the process at work:

> I know that I braid too much my own
> Snapped-off perceptions of things as they come to me.
> They are private and always will be.

Later on in "The One Thing That Can Save America," the poem I am quoting from, these private matters surface again as "the quirky things that happen to me."

Such things, central to the private energy that fuels the public poem, are its root force, but they clutter up the surface, effectively entangling us in Ashbery's own business of living. Nevertheless, because purely private material can in no conventional way be simplified by literary analysis, we are much better off experiencing it directly rather than trying to "understand" it. "Understanding," which most readers of poetry have been trained by generations of text-analyzers to believe is the object of reading, can be extracted from an Ashbery poem only at the price of distortion. What Ashbery offers instead is a chance for us vicariously to engage in something that might be called experiential process; he immerses us in a shifting context of unpredictable "meanings" and tones that constantly qualify everything that has gone before them yet that also are constantly qualified by everything that has been established.

Consider, for example, what happens to the phrases from "The Only Thing That Can Save America" when they are reinserted back into the poem. Because paraphrase in Ashbery is not just unnecessary but almost impossible, I'd like to quote the whole poem, pausing now and then to watch shifting tones operate rather than trying to make translations of phrases that are perfectly transparent once they are extracted from the amalgam of the poem. What I hope to reveal is nothing more than technique: Ashbery's method of confining meaning to the page, his system of preventing us from discovering a "solution" to something that is in fact not a riddle but an unsolvable work of art.

This poem that I have arbitrarily made central to my discussion is also almost literally central (pages 44 and 45 of an 83 page book) to *Self-Portrait in a Convex Mirror*, and centrality seems initially to be its central concern. The tone at the beginning is neutral, though phrases like "flung out" and "knee-high" force the reader into momentary minor adjustments of physical point of view:

> Is anything central?
> Orchards flung out on the land,
> Urban forests, rustic plantations, knee-high hills?
> Are place names central?
> Elm Grove, Adcock Corner, Story Book Farm?
> As they concur with a rush at eye level
> Beating themselves into eyes which have had enough
> Thank you, no more thank you.

Punning transformations of Stony Brook Farm and Alcott into Story Book and Adcock seem to put us either somewhere in the nineteenth century, on a thruway or possibly on railroad tracks, or in contemporary childhood; but the tone skids away from neutrality and toward a very clear petulance ("enough/ Thank you, no more thank you") as abruptly aggressive (and concurring) places threaten to gang up on the speaker:

> And they come on like scenery mingled with darkness
> The damp plains, overgrown suburbs,
> Places of known civic pride, of civil obscurity.

Again point of view has shifted, for we discover that the scenery we had accepted as "real" scenery is in fact only something that is "like scenery" in a commingling community of jumbled "civic pride" and "civil obscurity."

The second stanza brings us to the first flat assertion of the poem:

> These are connected to my version of America
> But the juice is elsewhere.

"The juice," of course, is private—most likely private energy—and though the tone is again close to neutral flatness (with perhaps an ironic pun on breakfast orange juice), it soon shifts into a rhapsodic lyricism:

> This morning as I walked out of your room
> After breakfast crosshatched with
> Backward and forward glances, backward into light,
> Forward into unfamiliar light,
> Was it our doing, and was it
> The material, the lumber of life, or of lives
> We were measuring, counting?
> A mood soon to be forgotten
> In crossed girders of light, cool downtown shadow
> In this morning that has seized us again?

Both time and perspective tangle in this complex scene that is like a painting but not one, a structure built of crosshatching glances in which the observing "I" is both active participant (and consequently invisible) and yet made visible to his own "downtown" memory as he thinks back on the significant moment. Able to be both in and out of the scene, he has no difficulty in translating the streaks of intersecting glances into an invisible pattern superimposed on light and then considering whether this might indeed be how "the lumber of life" is made significant (measured, counted). "Lumber" achieves a lovely suspension, forcing us to recollect the woods of the first stanza—orchards, forests, plantations, Elm Groves, overgrown suburbs—while at the same time anticipating the "crossed girders of . . . shadow" that will threaten to obliterate the morning that "has seized us again."

Crosshatched by glances, by planes of light, by simultaneously interior and exterior points of view, and by triple time (the opening statement's "objective" time, the "morning," and the "downtown" memory of morning that soon will be forgotten), the stanza's multiple perspectives present an "it" impossible to define and also impossible not to respond to.

It is at this stage in the poem's development that another neutral statement returns us to the passages I have already quoted.

> I know that I braid too much my own
> Snapped-off perceptions of things as they come to me.
> They are private and always will be.
> Where then are the private turns of event
> Destined to boom later like golden chimes
> Released over a city from a highest tower?
> The quirky things that happen to me, and I tell you,
> And you instantly know what I mean?
> What remote orchard reached by winding roads
> Hides them? Where are these roots?

By now something of the pattern of the poem should be apparent. Stanzas begin in something like a neutral tone, the speaker addressing what at least seems to be a general audience. But that audience, as in this third stanza, soon breaks up into quite private components—as well as the obvious "public" one. Here, for example, the generalized you becomes both Ashbery talking to himself and, by the seventh line, Ashbery addressing the "you" of the breakfast scene. His subject, however, is privacy and its relationship to something as public as music, painting, and poetry. And the abrupt shift in tone of the "golden chimes" question lets him move from a neutral tone to something very different that might capriciously be called oracular. It also lets him distance his material by shifting his statement into a totally different rhetoric—in this instance, a rhetoric that sounds suspiciously like that of Wallace Stevens. Critics—and, for that matter, uncritical readers—have a hard time with allusive echoes of this sort. That is, they can never be quite certain if the shifted "voice" is parodistic, referential, or perhaps even deferential. And there is always, of course, the possibility that the passage may not be deliberately allusive at all—simply a matter of Ashbery unintentionally sounding like another writer. (The last lines of the second stanza, the passage about the "crossed girders of light, cool downtown shadow/ In this morning that has seized us again," sound to my ear a good deal like passages in Hart Crane's poetry; and I am reasonably certain that the final stanza's "All the rest is waiting/ For a letter that never arrives" is supposed to trigger us into an "Ah, T. S. Eliot!" response. But what seems to me a Crane allusion may very well not be one; and my conviction that the last stanza's Eliot-like passage is a deliberate allusion tempts me —irrationally—to see the "roots" line of the third stanza as a faint echo of "The Waste Land.") Such "problems" seem to me ultimately unimportant. That is, the echo or even the possibility of echo is enough to distance the tone. Similarly distancing, the questions at the end of the third stanza force the opening stanza's "real" orchards into a metaphoric role. And distancing through language alone, language that is both serious and a little funny, "quirky things" have some kind of relationship to historical, geographical, and literary landscapes. Yet in spite of all of these distances, "I"—both as person and as writer—exist and exist in a present definable America.

The last stanza seems to me to reassemble the scattered tones of the first three. But precise meaning is carefully evaded. The poem is not a sermon:

> It is the lumps and trials
> That tell us whether we shall be known
> And whether our fate can be exemplary, like a star.
> All the rest is waiting

For a letter that never arrives,
Day after day, the exasperation
Until finally you have ripped it open not knowing what it is,
The two envelope halves lying on a plate.
The message was wise, and seemingly
Dictated a long time ago.
Its truth is timeless, but its time has still
Not arrived, telling of danger, and the mostly limited
Steps that can be taken against danger
Now and in the future, in cool yards,
In quiet small houses in the country,
Our country, in fenced areas, in cool shady streets.

"We" has by this time become an amalgam of Ashbery, the "you and I" of the second stanza, and the reader that the poem is addressed to; it will become explicitly in the last stanza America. But each "we" also exists separately.

Like the "quirky things" of the third stanza, the "star" that our fate might lead us to in the final one strikes me as rather funny—a cross between the theatrical and heavenly kind. And indeed the ominous Eliotic letter that "never arrives" also takes on faintly comic qualities when it is ripped open, its contents discovered to be "wise," its message warning of danger and of the steps that might be taken against that danger now and in the future both known and unknown.

Like much in Ashbery, funny and serious material coexist in one context. The tone of the last stanza grows, however, increasingly "concerned"; and if we never find out what the mysterious undelivered message is that we manage symbolically not to receive, to tear up, and yet to assimilate, we do have some sense of its urgency. It has something, of course, to do with the need for fences and for the walls of small houses, for places that are "cool"; but its "meaning"—like the "meaning" of the poem—is available only to the person who apprehends it without "knowing what it is."

I offer this non-reading of a poem as a demonstration of technique, but I hope it is also a warning against false readings. Happily, David Shapiro, whose own sense of the integrity of poetry is very strong, approaches Ashbery neither as New Critic nor as historian, but as fellow poet who himself works in modes similar to those used by Ashbery.

He asks us to recall what most of us have casually assimilated: the literatures of America and Europe, an awareness of the history of music and painting, a little knowledge of classical and contemporary physics. Using these tools, he helps us explore not the "meaning" of Ashbery's poetry but the sensibility that gives rise to it and the cultural context of which it is a most vital part.

His approach is unorthodox. His insights into the ways a major contemporary poet organizes his art give us a sense not just of the techniques used by John Ashbery but of a structural aesthetic drawn on by a whole generation of poets, painters, musicians, and sculptors.

Acknowledgments

Acknowledgment is made to John Ashbery for permission to quote from *Some Trees*, copyright © 1956 by John Ashbery; *The Double Dream of Spring*, copyright © 1966, 1967, 1968, 1969, 1970 by John Ashbery; and *Rivers and Mountains*, copyright © 1962, 1963, 1964, 1966 by John Ashbery.

Quotations from *Three Poems*, copyright © 1970, 1971, 1972 by John Ashbery and *Self-Portrait in a Convex Mirror*, copyright © 1972, 1973, 1974, 1975 by John Ashbery are reprinted by permission of John Ashbery and Viking Penguin Inc.

Quotations from *The Tennis Court Oath*, copyright © 1957, 1959, 1960, 1961, 1962 by John Ashbery, are reprinted by permission of Wesleyan University Press.

Quotations from *The Meaning of Meaning* by C. K. Ogden and I. A. Richards are reprinted by permission of Harcourt Brace Jovanovich, Inc.

Chapter 1, "The Meaning of Meaninglessness," first appeared in slightly different form under the title "Urgent Masks: An Introduction to John Ashbery's Poetry," in *Field* #5, copyright © 1971 by Oberlin College.

For epigraph quotations from Wallace Stevens, acknowledgment is made to Alfred A. Knopf, Inc.: six lines from "Prologues to What Is Possible" from *The Collected Poems of Wallace Stevens*, and two lines from "Adagia" from *Opus Posthumous*.

Abbreviations

Works by John Ashbery will be documented directly in the text. The following abbreviations will be used:

. . . . at once it struck me, what quality went to form a Man of Achievement especially in Literature & which Shakespeare possessed so enormously—I mean *Negative Capability*, that is when man is capable of being in uncertainties, Mysteries, doubts, without any irritable reaching after fact & reason—

—John Keats (Letter to George and Tom Keats)

Unreal, give back to us what once you gave:
The imagination that we spurned and crave.
—Wallace Stevens,
("To The One of Fictive Music")

As he travelled alone, like a man lured on by a syllable without
    any meaning,
A syllable of which he felt, with an appointed sureness,
That it contained the meaning into which he wanted to enter,
A meaning which, as he entered it, would shatter the boat and
    leave the oarsmen quiet
As at a point of central arrival, an instant moment, much or little,
Removed from any shore, from any man or woman, and needing
    none.

—Wallace Stevens,
("Prologues to What Is Possible")

The Mirror Staged

Master of those who do not know, who cannot know, yet must know and are never satisfied with the facilities of certainty, John Ashbery like Wallace Stevens is a Lucretian poet in the minimally explanatory mode. Ashbery's poetry may be regarded usefully as a precursor of Derrida's critique of a metaphysics of presence. Surely, American poetry has known in an explicit and implicit sense the devilish senselessness of language in humorous and elegiac tones. Ashbery's poetry is humorously and melancholically self-reflexive and sees itself as a provisional, halting critique of naive and degraded referential poetries. The sign in Ashbery's collages is eminently cut off from the world.

The poet does not speak, but constantly is involved in that mute science of Derrida's: grammatology. Ashbery deflates our expectation of sense, of presence, by giving us again and again the playful zone of *deferred sense*. There is an icy autocratic humiliation of the reader, who expects again and again a center, only to be decentered. Ashbery's abilities are thus beautifully negative, in the line of Keats's grandest remarks on the Negative Capability of the poet who does not reach out after dogmatic certainties. Ashbery, like Stevens, is master of those who do know they do not know. In this, paradoxically, his work may function, with our best poetries, as a decentering, Socratic, dialectical resource. Such autonomous poetry is an intransigent force in a late and stupefied world.

John Ashbery went from a period of neglect to a period of abuse and envy without a transitional period of appreciation and praise. Still, there is only one world, that world of poetry, after all. Ashbery doesn't always hold the mirror (even the convex mirror) up to Nature, and that enrages some local Calibans. But as Jackson Pollock said when asked why he didn't imitate Nature: I am Nature. Ashbery has always known that poetry was transreferential, as the great Russians, Pasternak and Khlebnikov, understood it. Like a staircase to no floor, Ashbery's poetry draws attention to itself, and by thus drawing attention to palpability it is in love with linguistic consciousness. Ashbery's poetry may be best understood as an homage to consciousness and a love song to language inside language. Criticism of contemporary poetry often makes one think of a choice between so-called open and closed forms—between an urn or a tree. Poetry, however, is an unpretentious emptiness, a well, not a well-wrought urn. Ashbery, avoiding the degraded public naturalisms, working in all forms, all modes, all moods, all persistent genres, and by dissolving genres in his own favorite medium—eraser fluid— reminds us of the foolishness of any facile choice. Ashbery's poetry, dominantly nonreferential, seems to give to our homelessness a local habitation and a name. Poets are not the unacknowledged legislators of the world. Poets create the world, as Thucydides created the Peloponnesian Wars.

Poetry does not reflect reality; it constitutes reality, the way an electric powerhouse station throws a new light upon an old city, by dint of that poem of which Benjamin Lee Whorf spoke, the linguistic-mathematical formulae of force. Ashbery's poetry may seem to be a reflection upon a reflection upon a reflection, but it is actually a creation upon a creation. A certain "ex nihilo" reigns over the ethics of the text. Barthes has spoken of that text in which meaning "absents" itself. Just so, Ashbery is interested in creating the most autonomous of worlds, a Schoenbergian systemics with a bare nostalgia for the high orders. One reads his surface only misguidedly if one thinks to commit merely the *orthodoxy* of paraphrase upon it. The poem is a form to be entered and a defensive form to be used, not a code in a war of cryptographers. Practical criticism of such a form must be akin to the architectural-rhetorical criticism of Roman Jakobson and the most mature formulations of the vigorous Russian Formalists. Such a critique must be musical in its bias, but with a constant attention to the shape of the tropes, the by now familiar metaphorical-metonymic poles. Ashbery is an intellectual musician, and the requisite criticism must be one displaying all tact to its polysemy. The charm of poetry is its antireferential sensuousness.

A subtle formalism must respond to a degraded sociologism that sees works of art as symptoms; an equally subtle historical mode must respond to a formalism that empties a work out of its social hungers. The passion of Shklovsky, Yakubinski and Mukarovsky was a passion that committed itself to works of antimimetic art. Adorno, too, could recommend the vital autonomous works of Schoenberg rather than the more positive pieces of a neoclassical eclectic like Stravinsky. The damaging aspect of much contemporary antiformalism is that it takes too easy targets and also lacks any way to deal compassionately with the complex works of modernism and the significant adventures of our own day. The darkest aspect of a modish formalism leads to and from a species of indifference and a heroizing of indifference, rather than to the vital differences of our truest works of relation.

A vital literary criticism might encompass both the meditative dialectic of a Paul de Man and the equally inspiriting tones of Meyer Schapiro in his investigations of the semiotics of art. The poem and the relations between poems must become a matter of the joys of influence. The best poetry of our day is, moreover, a form of literary criticism, both in drab and golden tones.

All of Ashbery's work of the 1970s has pleasures to offer but may logically seem to conclude in his soberly inconclusive and Proustian long work, "Self-Portrait in a Convex Mirror." This work initiated for the poet a period of awards and honors, including the Pulitzer Prize and the National Book Award, and one may well ask whether such a period is characterized by exoteric as opposed to esoteric experimentation. Luckily, to paraphrase Stevens, poetry has other reasons beside honors for its existence. "Self-Portrait" is a masterpiece, and lives alongside the other great long poems of Ashbery. The poem does not displace the early works, but it does offer us some of the reasons for speculating both on development and lack of development.

The title, "Self-Portrait in a Convex Mirror," has for some been too easily a way of seeing Ashbery caught up in a confession *or* expressionism. For others, the title is merely the title of one of Parmigianino's paintings. But the poet has been careful to permit his title to be both a reference to the painting, an *objet trouvé* as it were, and a precarious homage to self-reflexiveness. From the beginning of the poem to the end, the poet reenacts both a meditation upon the painting (as upon a skull in the Renaissance) and a meditation on the unfolding of his own vital poem. The poem enacts, moreover, a criticism of mimesis, because the mirror in both painting and poem is the one of difficulty and convexity. The reader is given the laborious Penelope-task of dealing with this web of unweaving.

One might well ask why Ashbery has selected Parmigianino, the great Mannerist, to be the center of his poem of de-center-

ing. It is our age that has reclaimed the movement of Mannerism, as the social historian Arnold Hauser reminds us. Mannerism is no longer to be thought of in the pejorative sense. For
Ashbery and modern art critics, it is the movement of art away
from classical norms toward the dissonance that counts. It is a
movement in art that not only distorts, but rescues the very
value of distortion. It is the movement in art that questions the
very foundations of art by constantly proposing the dissolution
of ancient dogma. In its bizarre suavity, its unrealities, its sudden discontinuities, its constant theatricality, its inordinate
fondness for framing devices, Mannerism no longer seems to us
anything but our central precursor. The elongated syntax of
Ashbery, his love of parenthesis and ellipsis, his sense of being
cut off from any direct treatment of Nature, his disequilibria,
his mottled textures, even his very preference for the Mannerists as a subject, his self-reflexiveness and high self-consciousness—all of these make Ashbery a Mannerist in the most
positive sense. The very length of the meditation, like an extreme Proustian sentence, reminds one of the extremism of the
Mannerists. But, to paraphrase an old political joke, extremism
in the service of poetry is no vice. Hauser reminds us that our
age of montage has best understood the values of the extreme
Mannerists.[1]

"Self-Portrait" is pressured by light iambic pentameter. This
is one of its most mature triumphs, on the one hand creating a
sense of almost prose massing of the words, on the other creating the almost professional "finish" of the metrical stress. The
prose massing is another Manneristic trick. We are deluded by
the quotations from Vasari, for example, and other professional
art critics such as Sydney Freedburg, into thinking that the
poem is a species of *Paterson*, a collage of prose elements. But
here the prose is selected to yield and transform itself into part
of the streamlined body of this poem. The whole poem is art

2. Parmigianino. "Self-Portrait in a Convex Mirror." Kunsthistorisches Museum (Vienna).

criticism and poetry combined and a refutation of any mere genre criticism of itself. It has become that more than mature thing, a melancholic Lucretian meditation upon itself.

Ashbery's usual configurations link aesthetic and erotic metaphors. And this poem, too, equates difficulty in art with erotic frustrations. The poem is found at last to be (and this perhaps too baldly summarizes the fruit of many readings it deserves) a love poem to the image seen within, image of artist-virtuoso and young artist, *solus* yet infinite within the mirror of speculation. In a Lacanian sense, the poem is one of endless narcissistic possibility and impossibility. But the important aspect, I think, is that all this is dwelt upon not with the tones of the usual psychopathology of our day and its too easy critique of narcissism, but with the tones of a kind of contemporary Proust, probing the very question of narcissism. This is the poet's triumphant if muted tone.

And so, we watch the poet use Vasari's praise of Parmigianino's "great art" in copying as a parodic exaltation of a reflection upon a reflection. The contemporary poet feels estranged from any simple mimesis. This long poem has seemed to some an almost neoclassical coming to terms for Ashbery with directness, but note that each strophe is like one further turning in the labyrinth. Ashbery has written the poem very much like the parodies of spiritual progress in *Three Poems,* reminding us constantly of what must be "sequestered," concealed, frustrated in attempts at mimesis. It might be said that the poem finally admits no self-portraiture except the portraiture of a text, a text like a painting. The poem often reveals this melancholy in contradiction: "The secret is too plain. The pity of it smarts,/ Makes hot tears spurt: that the soul is not a soul,/ Has no secret, is small" (SP, 69). To believe that one can escape the text, get out of it as into a realm of existence beyond language, is an impossibility filled with pathos: "One would like to stick one's hand/

Out of the globe, but its dimension,/ What carries it, will not allow it" (SP, 69).

And yet, for all this allegory of self-reflexiveness, the poet has subdominantly built up the theme of an almost random life attempting to intrude upon the seamless linguistic surface. Here, Ashbery tends to be less particular: "How many people came and stayed a certain time . . . Photographs of friends, the window and the trees . . ." (SP 71). It is the "strewn evidence" of the wreckage between the self and others. The self has been precise in constructing its own mirror, but so much less precise (though with a kind of "honesty") in constructing the difficult Other.

At one moment in "Self-Portrait," cities are named as the paradigmatic Baudelaire-like landscape in which these adventures with the Other take place. "Vienna where the painting is today, where/ I saw it with Pierre in the summer of 1959; New York . . ." (SP, 75). The poet has become his own *flaneur*, strolling through city streets to arrive at the museum where he can best see, at some length and with much dandyism, the tortured image, still so refreshing, of himself. He escapes from too much blurred impressionism by retreating into almost mathematical melancholies: "Where I am now, which is a logarithm/ Of other cities" (SP, 75). The poem is one of intransigent endurance in the face of inertia: "Can you stand it,/ Francesco? Are you strong enough for it?" (SP, 75). Here the poet, by speaking intimately to the portrait as to his second self, reminds us that the text and its self are not so imperious. The poet creates an *Ich-du* relation with his own web and in this way establishes not just a narcissism but an elementary relation. Self-reflexiveness, in "Self-Portrait," is finally about the health of uncertainty: "the normal way things are done,/ Like the concentric growing up of days/ Around a life: correctly, if you think about it." (SP, 76).

There is a tone somewhat of "Four Quartets" here, a tone of chastity rather than narcissism, of sanctity almost, as one finds it, peculiarly enough for some, in the jokes of John Cage and his Thoreau-like writings. Sensuality for our poet can never be dismissed, however: "Love once/ Tipped the scales but now is shadowed, invisible,/ Though mysteriously present, around somewhere" (SP, 77). Language is always already an eros.

In the last strophe of "Self-Portrait," as much as any other place in his poetry, Ashbery becomes the poet of pluralism *par excellence*. Like a more intimate Isaiah Berlin on Alexander Herzen, Ashbery speaks passionately against any reductive absolutism. "Each person/ Has one big theory to explain the universe/ But it doesn't tell the whole story . . ." (SP, 81). It is not that anyone else is going to spare us the agonies of aesthetic and ethical choice: "Yet I know/ That no one else's taste is going to be/ Any help" (SP, 82). Finally, Ashbery affirms particularity and the past, but understands with Proust and Keats that the true paradises are lost: "Once it seemed so perfect—gloss on the fine/ Freckled skin, lips moistened as though about to part/ Releasing speech" (SP, 82). "Releasing speech" is a fine emblem for the kind of satisfactions sought within and upon and truly inside language in this poem and all of Ashbery's oeuvre, which is always both prison-house and lost paradise. Any bare colloquial mimesis is barely the first step: "Aping naturalness." Art is both a veil interposed and proposition *toward* reality: "Offer it no longer as a shield or greeting,/ The shield of a greeting, Francesco." The so-called "self-consuming text" announces itself as properly suicidal: "There is room for one bullet in the chamber" (SP, 82). Poetry is slow suicide and slows down the suicidal.

"Self-Portrait in a Convex Mirror" does not permit the reader to think it is an aesthete's hookah-fantasy: "the 'it was all a dream'/ Syndrome, though the 'all' tells tersely/ Enough how it wasn't." The poet chooses the tense tactfully to affirm his visionary status with some glory: "We have seen the city" (SP, 82). But immediately it is a vision of horror and reduplication: "it is the gibbous/ Mirrored eye of an insect" (SP, 82–83).

There are many successes in Ashbery's work of the '70s. One should certainly mention the brilliant catalogues in his "The Vermont Notebook," at once a poem and a whole travelogue, a diary as a lyric, a lyric that can accept such an extreme measure as a cemetery-like listing of friends' names for over two pages. These names become one of the most horrific jokes in Ashbery; they present us with the terrible arbitrariness of all language, the names so distant from their seeming objects, torn from their place in everyone's dream of coherence. The names are arranged in the poem in an almost murderous act of "un-naming." In *Houseboat Days,* the grand variations called "Fantasia on 'The Nut Brown Maid' " render again the impossible distance between two voices, called by the convention of the old English ballad it apes and to which it pays homage: *He* and *She.* He and she were never so utterly similar and yet so far apart. And pronouns as "shifters" are shifty indeed. Poetry has indeed become, as Robert Delaunay said of art, something shattered as the fruit-dish of Cezanne.

And why? Because the truth itself has shattered into something relative and nomadic. Because our poetry now must be a self-portrait of poetry in the most shattering of mirrors. Because poetry can no longer rely on simple releasing speech, but must rely on the most complex *re-writing* of releasing speech.

It has seemed to me for a long time important to defend John Ashbery's poetry, even against his more intemperate admirers. His poetry is a model of our most difficult aesthetic desires. It is often combatted by those who would combat almost the whole history of a Mallarméan poetics. It is true that here I will often defend it almost too practically, by the so-called criticism of beauties, but that is one method I would also defend most earnestly. There is no way to avoid connoisseurship in these matters. While I am intent on pointing to his structures, and to the dynamic integrity of his thematics, I am aware of a need for what the painter Barnett Newman has called "passionate criticism." Ashbery's poetry deserves a practical polemic on his behalf. At another time, under the august sky of eternity, we will have a more eternal critique. Much of what I say "on behalf of" Ashbery may be found to be useful in understanding the poetries that to some extent surround or imbricate his poetry. While I understand Ashbery's rich integrity, I would never give it patriarchal status. Our criticism is too easily "freudened" as it is. While in this study he appears alone, he exists in the common world of collaborating poetries.

Ashbery's poems of the 1970s break down the usual opposition of criticism and creative work, subjective and objective modes. They remind us that Freud's work was novelistic just as Wordsworth's work was in a sense scientific. Ashbery wants the poem to be a trace of the mind tracing the poem. The poem remains an object, but an object constantly demanding subjectivity in the most demanding Kierkegaardian sense. The poem uses the autobiographical mode, because that is all we have. Criticism has deleted too much of this subjective element. Kierkegaard said that Hegel had left himself out. Ashbery also reminds us of Kierkegaard's remark that Hegel would have been a great philosopher if he had regarded his Logic as only one in a world of logics, and that, as it is now, Hegel is only a comedian of a systematics. Ashbery's work is a relentless tirade against systematics. For this reason, he is neither pure nor impure, neither art-for-art's-sake nor vulgarly mimetic. He is the great pluralist and combines pop art figuration with abstract expressionist dissolution. His poetry is a reconciliation, at its best, between the human subject and the inhuman workings of arbitrariness, between the fact of value and the value of fact. In a world too dominated by the psychological language of norms versus neuroses, Ashbery accepts the anomalous in himself and in language. He has made both his unhappiness and his ecstasy courageous topics in a world of topics. Unlike Stevens' lunatic of one idea, he is in love with *permission* and the earth and the earthiness of language and its unearthly arbitrariness.

If anyone wants to think that all this is merely what Yvor Winters deposed as a romantic mimesis of chaos, let him think again. The Tolstoy who created the richest works was the Tolstoy who could engulf man in libertine particularity, not the Tolstoy of a reductive absolutism. Ashbery's poetry has all the courage of the most defiant mimesis and antimimetic music. At no time does he merely represent chaos, and at all times his burden, "the burden of the mystery" in Keats's phrase, is gracefully carried.

Ashbery's best work, like the paintings of Jasper Johns, seems an intelligent if dark confrontation with the forces of the given. For Johns, the given may be an alphabet, target, flag, or map. For Ashbery, it is the world of degraded and charming cliché, doggerel, bad taste, Hollywood convention, newspaper prose, literary pietism, and metaphysical jargon. The central metaphysical-moral component in Ashbery's verse is its deadly withdrawal of the transcendental term and insistence on individual liberty. His image of the world does not lead to an hedonism pursued along the lines of an American pragmatic, though his ideas are as clear as a pragmatist's. He might agree with Charles Pierce that man is a sign. Ashbery's poetry, moreover, leads, as we have seen, through an excruciating evaluation of the possible consolations, cognitive and sensual, that are available. The poem is a difficulty, a resistance, and a critique. The final consolation for the poet may be, as with Stevens, the imagination. An imagination not of fragrance or of stippled sensibility nor of a late, bare, philosophical, and perhaps deluded penetration to *realia,* as in early and late Stevens. The imagination in Ashbery speaks of a constantly agitated *agon* in which the poet has only the paradoxia of what Leonard Foerster has called "the poetry of significant nonsense" in Morgenstern and Ball. Man is locked in the unintelligible or barely intelligible labyrinth of language; one's art is forced to remain repetitive and solipsistic, and yet somehow adventurous. In discontinuous streams, in mistranslations, in suburban resentments and urban uncertainties, in action poetry, Ashbery leads ambiguity to the verge of nonsense and keeps it satisfactorily unredeemed.

A dictionary of clichés is not a cliché. In Ashbery's work there is neither unmastered nor mastered irony. There is the constant process of *mastering irony.* The opposite of poetry is not prose or science, but stupidity.

CHAPTER 1

The Meaning of Meaninglessness

Some movement is reversed and the urgent masks
Speed toward a totally unexpected end
Like clocks out of control. Is this the gesture
That was meant, long ago, the curving in

Of frustrated denials . . .
("Song," *The Double Dream of Spring*)[1]

. . . But there was no statement
At the beginning. There was only a breathless waste,
A dumb cry shaping everything in projected
After-effects orphaned by playing the part intended for them,
Though one must not forget that the nature of this
Emptiness, these previsions
Was that it could only happen here, on this page held
Too close to be legible, sprouting erasures, except that they
Ended everything in the transparent sphere of what was
Intended only a moment ago, spiraling further out, its
Gesture finally dissolving in the weather.
("Clepsydra," *Rivers and Mountains*)[2]

John Ashbery once took a course of lectures in music by Henry Cowell at the New School. Ashbery recalls Cowell remarking that the intervals in music become wider as music grows more sophisticated: "for instance, if you compare 'The Volga Boatmen' and the 'Love Duet' in *Tristan und Isolde* you see how vastly wide the intervals have become; and the ear seemingly becomes accustomed to unaccustomed intervals, 'as time goes by' " (interview).[3] One cannot really anticipate the next note in many serial pieces, and this suspense is a fine quality of Ashbery's own work and a theme:

> These decibels
> Are a kind of flagellation, an entity of sound
> Into which being enters, and is apart.
> Their colors on a warm February day
> Make for masses of inertia, and hips
> Prod out of the violet-seeming into a new kind
> Of demand that stumps the absolute because not new
> In the sense of the next one in an infinite series
> But, as it were, pre-existing or pre-seeming in
> Such a way as to contrast funnily with the unexpectedness
> And somehow push us all into perdition.
>
> ("The Skaters," RAM, 34)

When Ashbery interviewed Henri Michaux for *Art News*, the French fabricator of imaginary communities spoke of surrealism as *une grande permission*, in the sense of an army leave (interview). However, surrealism tends to be used and abused; as in the case of Robert Bly, who tends to exaggerate certain overblown qualities of Spanish surrealism. Ashbery's surrealism is subtler. Raymond Roussel's flat, bland, and objective style, typified by Ashbery as "French as one is taught to write it by manuals in lycées" (interview), a French that can comically be compared to *Larousse*, has been a minor if decided influence.

Ashbery was a connoisseur of Roussel and began a doctoral dissertation on him but decided not to go through with it, although characteristically he collected many minute particulars about that grand eccentric. Thus the modulated parodies of narration in *Rivers and Mountains* may be associated with the labyrinthine parentheses of Roussel's poems and novels; this contagion of the parodistic tone seems to lead structurally to a "chinese box" effect or play within a play. Besides this parenthetical mania, other idiosyncrasies of Roussel, the author of *Locus Solus*, did not impinge on the early work of Ashbery, who did not read him thoroughly until the 1950s, which he spent in France (interview). Later Ashbery wittily employed another device of Roussel: the specious simile, "The kind that tells you less than you would know if the thing were stated flatly" (interview). In lieu of the organic and necessary simile, Ashbery learned from the French master an extravagance of connection that leads one nowhere, as in "as useless as a ski in a barge," though this example is perhaps still too suggestive. "As useless as a ski" would be Ashbery's paradigmatic revision (interview). Ashbery is also a master of the false summation, the illogical conclusion couched in the jargon of logic and reminiscent of the false but rich scholarship of Borges:

We hold these truths to be self-evident:
That ostracism, both political and moral, has
Its place in the twentieth-century scheme of things;
That urban chaos is the problem we have been seeing into and seeing
    into,
For the factory, deadpanned by its very existence into a
Descending code of values, has moved right across the road from total
    financial upheaval
And caught regression head-on. . . .

.   .   .

To sum up: We are fond of plotting itineraries
And our pyramiding memories, alert as dandelion fuzz . . .
                                    ("Decoy," DDS, 31)

The rise of capitalism parallels the advance of romanticism
And the individual is dominant until the close of the nineteenth cen-
    tury.
In our own time, mass practices have sought to submerge the personal-
    ity
By ignoring it, which has caused it to branch out in all directions . . .

                    .   .   .

And yet it results in a downward motion, or rather a floating one . . .
                            ("Definition of Blue," DDS, 53–54)

John Ashbery can properly be called a child of the muse of
Rimbaud. In the somewhat unenthusiastic tones of the introduction to *Some Trees*,[4] W. H. Auden also placed him in the
tradition of Rimbaud's *dérèglement de tous les sens.* Contrary to
Auden's expectations, Ashbery denies French poetry as a major
influence. He does, however, acknowledge the influence of
Pierre Reverdy, whom he read as a "simple poet" accessible to
a student with limited French; he later translated some of Reverdy's cubist concoctions. He admires "the completely relaxed,
oxygen-like quality of Reverdy," whose cadences he likens to
"breathing in big gulps of fresh air" (interview). René Char's
war journals, which did not intrigue Ashbery, are similar in
their impersonality in that they command so many styles of
expression.

Raymond Roussel, one of the minor French influences, is a
very "prosy" poet, and Ashbery also is interested in the poetic
possibilities of conventional and banal prose, the prose of newspaper articles. Many of his poems of the '60s and '70s are particularly works that function by proceeding from cliché to cliché,
in a "seamless web" of banality transformed, by dint of combi-

nation and deformation, into a Schwitters-like composition in which the refuse of a degraded quotidian is fused into a new freshness:

> It is never too late to mend. When one is in one's late thirties, ordinary things—like a pebble or a glass of water—take on an expressive sheen. One wants to know more about them, and one is in turn lived by them. Young people might not envy this kind of situation, perhaps rightly so, yet there is now interleaving the pages of suffering and indifference to suffering a prismatic space that cannot be seen, merely felt as the result of an angularity that must have existed from earliest times and is only now succeeding in making its presence felt through the mists of helpless acceptance of everything else projected on our miserable, dank span of days. . . . The pain that drained the blood from your cheeks when you were young and turned you into a whitened specter before your time is converted back into a source of energy that peoples this world of perceived phenomena with wonder.
>
> ("The New Spirit," *Three Poems*)[5]

The use of prose elements in poetry, as in William Carlos Williams and Ezra Pound, is so common a heritage and so diffused a technique as rarely to provoke sensations of novelty, but Ashbery's intense employment is an adventure. The prosaic elements in the early poetry of W. H. Auden influenced Ashbery, as did the touching qualities of ordinary speech, journalism, and old diaries in Auden's *The Orators* (interview). Collage elements for Ashbery's poem "Europe" were taken from a book for girls written at the time of the First World War. The book, William LeQueux's *Beryl of the Bi-Planes,* which he picked up by accident on one of the quais of Paris, is one reason for much of the placid plane imagery of "Europe" (interview). At the time, Ashbery was "collaging" a great deal as a symptom of an imagined "dead-end" period in his writing; living in France, he felt cut off from American speech (interview). He often received

American magazines and manipulated their contents as a stimulus and pretext for further poetry. The grand collapses often noted in Ashbery's "Europe," its dashes and discontinuities, are one result of this *collagiste* direction. Though Ashbery's poetry leads most recently to a calm clearness, it truly began with the presentation of "objects" and "idioms" in explicitly dislocated form:

> sweetheart . . . the stamp
>   ballooning you
> vision I thought you
> forget, encouraging your vital organs.
> Telegraph. The rifle—a page folded over.
>
> More upset, wholly meaningless, the willing sheath
>   ("Europe," *The Tennis Court Oath*)[6]

His dislocated poetry had something of the pathos of obscurity, and the "pathos of incomprehensibility" was very much part of the mystique of such writing, though Ashbery always pointed towards principles of cohesion by discontinuity, if using the concealments of riddle and hints:

> She was dying but had time for him—
> brick. Men were carrying the very heavy things—
>   dark purple, like flowers.
> Bowl lighted up the score just right
>   ("Europe," TCO, 68)

Gertrude Stein furnished a specimen source for the opacities of "Europe" (interview). But Ashbery has a very full palette, and one must distinguish between grammatical anomaly, unexpected dream imagery, and the nonsensical. Ashbery is one of the poets who senses an epoch's rule system for sense itself and revolts against it with wit. His theme of "unacceptability" is allied always to related concepts of absurdity, stupidity, and the unreal.

There are a plethora of analogues in the associated arts. At the time Ashbery was writing as art editor for the *Herald Tribune International Edition*, de Kooning, Kline, and Pollock, with extreme dash and discontinuity, were calling attention to the expunging of the *copula* and the coherent figure; they were calling attention to the theme of composition itself. Later the New Realists, the Pop Artists of France, were to revive Duchamp's abrupt presentation of everyday objects. The self-conscious mid-progress shifts of narration in Ashbery's *collagiste* poems, moreover, are distinctly and masterfully of the age in which Jackson Pollock threw himself on the canvas, a proof and *permission*. Even though Ashbery unexpectedly characterizes himself as more aural than visual, his participation in the art world as critic has been a constant source for his critical poetry.

The influence of psychoanalysis, also, permitting a more or less watery relationship with the unconscious and everyday mind, and corollary devices of "dipping into" an almost completely associational stream ("What else is there?" [interview]) is another common heritage of technique Ashbery shares with the abstract expressionists and surrealists. The Arthur Cravan translations in *The Double Dream of Spring* (pp. 61–65) were interesting to Ashbery largely because he felt they resembled certain associational, disjunct narrations that he had already achieved (interview). Ashbery has called attention to more than one neglected poet, and as a matter of fact once considered editing a kind of *Anthology of Neglected Poets* (interview). In this hypothetical anthology of idiosyncratic tastes, Ashbery considers John Wheelwright, David Schubert, Samuel Greenberg, and the British poet F. T. Prince as bizarre cousins or in-laws, all applying the same "syntax of dreams" for dramatistic purposes (interview).

Ashbery's work, begun with kinds of *disjecta membra*, co-alesces at certain periods in big coherent works: "Europe," "The Skaters," "The New Spirit," "The System," and "The Re-cital." The development from collage of seemingly despairing fragments to unbroken paragraphs of de Chirico-like prose (Ash-bery admits to de Chirico's prose and not painting as an influ-ence [interview]) is likened, by the author, to the development of one of Ashbery's favorite composers, Busoni. "Busoni wrote a piano concerto, entitled 'The Turning Point,' and all his sub-sequent music fittingly seems different from earlier pieces" (in-terview). Similarly in Ashbery's poetry the disjointed and in-decisive has the look, at least, of a highly unified music. Ashbery's larger compositions achieve this "look" of composi-tional unity while remaining what may be a "multeity." Com-position in these works is not random but rather more a matter of parsimonious distribution of disparate images, tones, and parodies than of unifications and harmonizings. One may find a tone of Pope in "The Skaters," and the mock-heroic here does sometimes bear resemblance to the highly polished surface of *The Rape of the Lock*. The highly polished surface in Ashbery, however, is less a social hint than a *memento mori* of a world of manufactured objects and smooth, unbroken concrete. "The Skaters" may be thought of as a radiant porphyry of a variety of rhetorics, including imitations of Whitman, Baudelaire, science textbooks, translations of Tu Fu, Theodore Roethke, and John Ashbery. He has described his intentions in respect to "The Skaters" as trying "to see how many opinions I had about every-thing" (interview). The most alarming feature of this style is the way it keeps upsetting our charming equilibrium and under-standing of tone. After a quaint satire on the classic Oriental story of the failing student, Ashbery announces: "The tiresome old man is telling us his life story" (RAM, 63). To some, his meditations upon or within meditations of self-laceration add to the absurdity of the universe rather than interpret it, but these are ultimately friendly satires which point to the fact that unity, as we dream of it, is not realizable. One dreams of the perfect language within the fallen universe. Ashbery's deceptive drifts and accumulations of parody always erupt in the dramatic return which surprises and regulates, as in Proust. By his grand multeity in unity, his surprising simultaneity in unity, and a type of probabilistic unity, he achieves something of the misery and joy of a Jacques Callot baroque. He has always avoided the vanity that derives from purely random techniques. But the spectre of indeterminacy and uncertainty shadow his structural convolutions and involutions, if only in the numerous self-lacerating dwarfs that appear and disappear throughout his poems.

Ashbery called my attention to a discussion of reticence by Margaret Atwood in *Field* (No. 4): "I don't want to know how I write poetry. Poetry is dangerous. I believe most poets will go to any lengths to conceal their own reluctant scanty insight both from others and from themselves. Paying attention to how you do it is like stopping in the middle of any other totally involving and pleasurable activity to observe yourself suspended in the fatally suspended inner mirror" (p. 70). Ashbery has been most extreme in his reluctance to pad his poetry with what he calls the "stuff of explanation," just as he has been reluctant to be anything but a "practical critic" or "anecdotal" critic of the arts (interview). However, one of his central themes is the breakdown of causality in the nineteenth-century sense. His discontinuities tend to throw us most clearly into the middle of the century of the Uncertainty Principle, one in which the poet and scientist expunge false *copulas* for a truer style. The montages of Eisenstein and Ezra Pound's clear, cinematic Oriental translations are part of this lucid tradition of juxtaposition. Most of the best passages in Ashbery's poetry, moreover, as in Stevens' work, still deal with the practitioner's point of view and *praxis* itself, however veiled. His poetry, though not vulgarly explanatory is, in the manner of the "action" painters, a criticism of poetry itself as much as of life. A dice-playing God does indeed reign over the aesthetics of Ashbery's kingdom.

Ashbery's first book, *Some Trees,* is already filled with revitalizations of forms that had become connotatively encrusted. His sestina, "The Painter" (1948, p. 54), is one of Ashbery's playfully formal structures and is influenced by Elizabeth Bishop. Her sestina, "A Miracle for Breakfast," employed such common end-words, such as coffee and balcony, that it charmed him (interview), and certainly the meticulously comical, soft-voiced rhetoric in Ashbery's own poetry shows the rapport between them. The sestina form, therefore, with its arbitrary and sometimes comically stiff canon, is a fitting "receptacle" for the play of discontinuity and *copula.* Ashbery's sestinas, as opposed to the more coherent ones of W. H. Auden and Ezra Pound, make much of a purposeful barrage of the unusual mid-progress shifts and blurred drama. Another example of disjointed and spiky writing within rigid form is the eclogue published in *Turandot:* [7]

> Cuddie: I need not raise my hand
> Colin: *She burns the flying peoples*
> Cuddie: To hear its old advice
> Colin: *And spears my heart's two beasts*
> Cuddie: Or cover with its mauves
> Colin: *And I depart unhurt*

"This poem was written after a bleak period of unproductiveness in 1962, when I was in publishing. I was somewhat awakened by a concert of John Cage's music" (interview). This music, more than anything then happening in painting, shook him and seemed to give him, once more, the *"permission"* to find a form in the fertile formlessness into which he had wandered.

There is a kind of simultaneous irony and depth to Ashbery's work, as if a critic paused to announce that he was invalidating all his critical statements including the present one he was making and yet continued. His simultaneity is also that of chamber music, in which the "narration" of four voices can seem, as in Haydn, to recreate the comic possibilities of a domestic quarrel over a dish-towel. His domesticity and Firbankian penchant for prosy gossip can be seen further enlarged in his collaborative venture, *A Nest of Ninnies*.[8] His "Pantoum" (ST, 30), inspired by Ravel, is another example of a witty use of an arbitrary and musical form. Again, it is music, not the rhyming dictionary (though see his "Variations, Calypso and Fugue on a Theme of Ella Wheeler Wilcox" [DDS, 24–26] for some canny couplets) that inspires Ashbery's poetry. He is averse to "melodious poetry" though not to melody itself. He is most interested in sound as it joins and flies apart from the meaning of the words, and his disjunction is reminiscent of Anton Webern's practice of setting a poem with a meagre amount of imitative music. Busoni's music appeals to Ashbery in the sense that the notes, in his judgment, seem to be implying that they could be "any notes and they just happen to sound this way" (interview). Opposed to the pedanticism of Reger and the synthetic cubism of Schoenberg, the music of Busoni seems to Ashbery to enjoy the double status of generating a new grammar and then commenting on it (interview).

One must remark, if parenthetically, that though Ashbery's own intellectual music is associated journalistically with Frank O'Hara and Kenneth Koch, the discrimination of their differences is equally useful. At first they were pragmatically and conspiratorially joined against poets of a different aesthetic (Richard Wilbur, for example); but though they share a common *tradition* of French surrealism, a taste for the Russian poets of revolution, Pasternak and Mayakovsky, and a somewhat similar procedure of montage, the characteristic Ashbery tone is not that of the others. He is neither as celebratory as Koch nor as urbane and political as O'Hara. To lump the poets of the so-called "New York School" as contemporary Chaucerians is inaccurate. The meditations of Ashbery are piously pluralist, perhaps impious to some.

As for the subject of poetic influence, Ashbery has indeed digested both the influence of Wallace Stevens and Walt Whitman. He particularly loved the long poems of Stevens, "on which I wrote a paper [not extant] for F. O. Mathiessen at Harvard" (interview). His own ubiquitous third-person narrator might very well have derived from Wallace Stevens as a way of "entering" the poem. The dreamlike imagery of Ashbery's "He" (ST, 60), however, does indeed derive from a veritable dream. Much of the clumsy appropriateness of dreams is imitated in Ashbery's poems, though the flat lyrical catalogues of "Grand Abacus" (ST, 32) derive from the long lines of Whitman. Ashbery is "more spellbound by the technical virtuosity of Whitman than the spontaneous image of the bard mumbling in his beard" (interview). Ashbery's marvelous catalogues—like that of musical instruments in "The Skaters" (RAM, 35)—also derive from Webern's "Cantata," where things "go bumping and rumbling for a time after you thought they were going to stop" (interview). Certain elements of Ashbery's *catalogue raisonné* also can be associated with the noisiness of Whitman's poetry and prose.

True, melodious tolling does go on in that awful pandemonium,
Certain resonances are not utterly displeasing to the terrified eardrum.
Some paroxysms are dinning of tambourine, others suggest piano room
    or organ loft
For the most dissonant night charms us, even after death. This, after
    all, may be happiness: tuba notes awash on the great flood, ruptures
    of xylophone, violins, limpets, grace-notes, the musical instrument

called serpent, viola da gambas, aeolian harps, clavicles, pinball machines, electric drills, que sais-je encore!

("The Skaters," RAM, 35)

Ashbery says: "John Cage taught me the relevance of what's
there, like the noise now of those planes overhead" (interview).
However, he would hardly imagine the sole strategy of his poetry to be the capture of a probabilistic everyday, no matter
how prehensile the poet. His poetry sees the everyday in its
relation to the supreme moment, the in-between moment, the
pedestrian moments, and, Ashbery adds, "one cannot really
overlook any of them" (interview). Ashbery's divinely drab modulations, his equitably and imperturbably distributed polariza-
tions between these instants might lead one to the delusion that
this is a poetry of no terror. But it is actually more intense than
decorative, and while rococo in parts, it has much of T. S.
Eliot's anxious quick shifts of pose. It is not merely a deliquescence into an *Exercice du Style* along the lines of Raymond
Queneau. It is a less whimsical palette of possibilities.

Certain of the poems, "Clepsydra" (RAM, 27) for instance,
combine the brooding flatness of a meditative tone with some
almost impenetrable details of landscape. Ashbery admits to
having the experience, not of a vague rhythm but of a vague
vision previous to a poem. "Clepsydra" was favorably foreseen
as a "big slab, with no stanza breaks and like a marble slab down
which a little water trickles" (interview). The feeling tone of the
poem is not equally stony, for a lot of terrified exaltation of the
prosaic goes on. In "Clepsydra" he utilizes a repetition of "after
all" as a replica of a horrifying hack journalistic digression:

. . . It had reduced that other world,
The round one of the telescope, to a kind of very fine powder or dust
So small that space could not remember it.
Thereafter any signs of feeling were cut short by

The comfort and security, a certain elegance even,
Like the fittings of a ship, that are after all
The most normal things in the world. Yes, perhaps, but the words
"After all" are important for understanding the almost
Exaggerated strictness . . .

                                                    (RAM, 30)

He also refines a kind of legalistic diction, as in: "And it was in
vain that tears blotted the contract now, because/ It had been
freely drawn up and consented to as insurance . . ." (RAM,
30). One thinks of the sweet transpositions of legal diction in
Renaissance arguments. Surely, here too is a poetry ready to be
accused of yoking disparate tones and images with difficulty
together. Samuel Johnson's criticism of the Metaphysical poets
applied here tends to falter under the steady and sensible pres-
sure of Ashbery's thoughtful and feeling lines. Here, the strange
connections are the imagination unfolding itself.

Though classic parody has a target, these modulated parodies
do not quite break their lance against ignorance or excess; they
are targetless parodies which attempt to annihilate the idea of
parody, since parody is, for Ashbery, "almost an indecent idea"
(interview). The poet is interested in flattening out all parodistic
devices, using multiple and shifting targets of parody to blur the
Bergsonian function of intimidating the inelastic target. Ashbery
tries successfully to reinstate the poetic qualities of all possible
sources—journalism, degraded ditties, bad poetry—by implying
that there is no such thing as *the poetic*. His poems are not
ready-mades, as in the tradition of Marcel Duchamp, and he
feels "little kinship with Duchamp, who was a supremely glamorous negation of everything" (interview). Ashbery negates everything so that "we can go on to what is left" (interview). The
urinal of Duchamp is a witty negation of art, but Ashbery is trying merely to engulf that negation among many (thus, the frag-

ments of ready-made poetry within his poetry). He finds too many supreme culminations and duplicate negations of everything Duchamp did in today's art and literature (interview). His mature work, "The System," (TP) is couched in the clichés of devotional and pseudodevotional writing, and Ashbery gives an impressionistic criticism of its intent: "Just as one may be depressed by reading the fine print in the 11th edition of the *Encyclopedia Brittanica*, with long prose passages in eight point type, and feel as if one is drowning in a sea of unintelligible print—and yet this is one's favorite ocean, just as drowning is said to be delicious when one stops struggling, so I tried to reproduce that delicious sensation" (interview). His poetry starts with the feeling of cliché, the banal, the given, but ends with something complex and strange: disastrous relations.

One must also mention that new ways of writing a poetic prose were opened for Ashbery by the novel *Hebdomeros*[9] of de Chirico. This is another example of what he regards as neglected work of high quality. Ashbery was admittedly moved by the interminable digressions and flourishes of de Chirico, whose prose tends to burst out in terribly long sentences that go on for pages, and whose novels have but one character. The *skena* may change several times in de Chirico's sentences, as in Ashbery's, and the course of this sentence is as a cinematic flow, under which the writer is pushing further and further ahead, though camouflaged by one of those "urgent masks," which may be a parody of an ancient voice, such as Sir Thomas Browne's.

Ashbery's own work is much concerned with a true solicitude for the bitter impressions of meaninglessness, and this poetry which speaks of the fundamental religious absence of our day should certainly be appraised for what it is rather than for what it is not. After all, with its flourescent imagery, disjunction, collages, two-dimensionalisms, innovations in the traditional forms of sestina, and "simultaneous" use of an aggregate of styles, John Ashbery's poetry today constitutes a revitalization movement in American poetry.

Ashbery's poems are unclear; they are mysterious and seem meant to be so. Throughout this study, I shall attempt to show *how* they are unclear, and how Ashbery values the unclear, and what is gained and lost by this species of opacity. Some of the poems are filled with dissociated elements that teasingly suggest different meanings. Humor is a large element throughout Ashbery's work: the humor of polysemy.

The poet tends to use paradox and "nonsense" to achieve, not so much an ambiguity of the kind analyzed denotatively and connotatively by "The New Critics," as a pointing to *logos* by its extreme absence. This theme of the absence of meaning and a concomitant style of concealments and opacities is the central and abiding metaphor within the specimen texts. As critics have explored and "rescued" the genre of pornography, so I shall attempt to re-value the neo-Dadaist works of Ashbery, by stylistic analysis, metaphrasis, and interdisciplinary analogues. One finds that his techniques of dissociation, his use of the banal, the antipoetic, the discontinuous, and the arbitrary all yield clues to possible states of wholeness. I view the work of the '70s, moreover, as the extreme attempt to escape from the bleaker aspects of "the unacceptable" in "nonsense" and to calculate the possibility of a conversion to the heavy requirements of love and belief, which are however mercilessly parodied.

One might take the famous catalogue of I. A. Richards and C. K. Ogden [10] and disrupt their definitions of *meaning* to indicate what a palette of "meaninglessness" might be, and how congruent this is with the central theme and style of Ashbery. If "meaning is an intrinsic property," [11] meaninglessness in Ashbery's work is conjured up by an utter denial of intrinsic *logos*, by his lacerations of any such pathetic fallacy in his "colorless indifferent universe" (interview).

If meaning is "a unique unanalysable relation to other things" (*Meaning*, p. 186), then meaninglessness in Ashbery is evoked by the constant scrutiny of disrupted rapports and the loss of any coherent relation between Nature, Man, and Divinity. If connotation is meaning, then Ashbery's poetry, like Gertrude Stein's, attempts utter meaninglessness by attempting to strip the word of any of its usual configurations and connotations.

If meaning is an "essence," then Ashbery like Sartre is existentialist and presents an absurdist impasse without essence. If meaning is "an event intended" (*Meaning*, p. 186) then Ashbery takes from the world this species of coherence by presenting a world of blank contingency, funny and unfunny unexpectedness.

If meaning is the place of anything in a system, Ashbery evokes a world where "the system" is almost an utterly unsystematic stream in which usual places, indeed any *locus*, is seen to be deprived. Only an absence of locus remains, as in the astronomer's concept of an extremely weighty black hole.

If meaning is "practical consequences" (*Meaning*, p. 186) then Ashbery by dint of *non sequitur* tends to shatter any sense of causality. The fallacy of *post hoc propter hoc* is ridiculed endlessly and seen to lead only into a world of old-fashioned sentiment and false coherence.

If meaning is "emotion aroused by anything," Ashbery's flatness attempts an affectless pose and poise to lance the sense of any arousal or emotion. If meaning is "what anything Suggests" (*Meaning*, p. 187), Ashbery often attempts paradoxically to suggest "nothing," to present a blank configuration of words in which any interpretation may be an overinterpretation, and the circumference of meaning is either seen to be zero or practically infinite.

If meaning is "that to which the User of a Symbol refers," Ashbery is peculiarly evocative of meaninglessness when he tries to employ words without a seeming concern for the referential, as in his collaged bits and fragments. The white spaces between his words seem to remain as suggestively referential as the words themselves, with the whole pointing mystically, or insidiously, nowhere.

If meaning is that "to which the user of a symbol Ought to be referring," then Ashbery mocks the reader into a meaninglessness of an antinomian bent by consistently employing a theme that tends against any but the most chaotic obligations. Experimentalism, metrical betrayals, betrayals of syntax: all go to show that Ashbery rejects this category of "meaning."

If meaning is, finally, "that to which the interpreter of a symbol either refers, or believes himself to be referring, or believes the User to be referring" (*Meaning*, p. 187), then Ashbery's "puzzle pictures" lead maddeningly into a labyrinth of possible denotations and possible lack of denotations.

These are some of the meanings of meaninglessness. In Ashbery's poetry, there is much confidence in a new threshold for incoherence and randomness, leading to affirmations of freedom. The poet avoids any transcendental defense for his usages of contingency, but in his work order is wilfully and painstakingly rescued from disorder. Conventional orders and meanings are parodied sharply and starkly.

The following study is intended as an introduction and "guide to the perplexed" for the readers in Ashbery's difficult work, and it privileges the texts I find most radical, most audacious in Pasternak's sense that "the root of beauty is audacity." *The Double Dream of Spring*, for example, with its pastoral perfections, has gained already perhaps an adequate hermeneutics. My concentration is on the neglected or problematic texts that I find most fruitful or difficult. The bulk of this book is devoted to analyses, sometimes metaphrastic, of the major books by the poet. The early work is treated as significant, crystalline, if derivative work. The second period, that of *The Tennis Court Oath*, is treated more intensely, with an extended study of the collage-poem "Europe" (TCO). Since Ashbery's work tends to coalesce in significant, synthetic masterpieces, his mature meditation "The Skaters" (RAM, 34) is given an extended analysis and appraisal. *Three Poems* (1972), curiously opaque, is shown as a fine and mature step in the conversion of the poet from an exquisite *collagiste* to a poet of some moral order and authority. He has gained authority in all of his work of the '70s because of his tolerance for negativity.

CHAPTER 2

The Early Work

Ashbery's early work is significant for its preponderance of dream imagery. It is in later Ashbery that we have a sustained meditation on the quotidian and an escape from early escapism and phantasmagoria. In the early work the operation of the sleeping consciousness is delineated, and there is a sacrifice of the everyday made in the direction of Arthur Rimbaud, the French symbolists and surrealists in general, and Wallace Stevens. Instead of the homogeneous prose parodies of the later Ashbery, one has formal texts, with a variety of metrical or quasimetrical devices, as in the sestina, "The Painter" (ST, 54). The early work is disjunct, but less so than the collages of the late 1950s. The central emphasis is not yet on the banal, the ready-made, and forms of disbelief, but on dream landscape and delicate dislocations.

"Two Scenes" in *Some Trees* (p. 9) contains an obvious dream landscape: " 'We see you in your hair/ Air resting around the tips of mountains' " (ST, 9). The dreamlike blurring of "hair" and "air" with its sudden and unexpected rhyme is a typical technical "aberration" of the early work. The shift in scene and the shift to rhyme in betrayal of the unrhymed norm is comparable to a dream's quick transitions: "This is perhaps a day of general honesty/ Without example in the world's history/ Though the fumes are not of a singular authority/ And indeed are dry as poverty" (p. 9). Part of the humor of the early Ashbery is his modestly quiet employment of these off-rhymes within an unrhymed norm.

The early work of Ashbery often explores sexual ambiguities in a fractured narrative. A good example is the sudden eroticization in the poem, "Popular Songs" (ST, 10):

> He continued to consult her for her beauty
> (The host gone to a longing grave).
> The story then resumed in day coaches
> Both bravely eyed the finer dust on the blue. That summer
> ("The worst ever") she stayed in the car with the cur.
> That was something between her legs

The use of businesslike questions ("and what about the net rest of the year?" [ST, 10]) juxtaposed with the sexual tension of the poem creates a comical disjunction. The lyric is filled with the vivid color of dreams or eidetic imagery: "guano-lightened summer night landscape" (ST, 10). The slightly comical colors are also adapted to the banal rhymes that lead toward the closure: "You laugh. There is no peace in the fountain./ The footmen smile and shift. The mountain/ Rises nightly to disappointed stands" (ST, 10).

"Eclogue" is an early example of Ashbery pursuing the archaic for its own sake (ST, 12). The formula of pastoral dialogue is used, not for any common idyllic purposes, but for a dream dialogue with violent, seemingly nonsensical shifts. The syntax is not anomalous, as in later Ashbery, but the imagery seems certainly anomalous: "And there, spiked like some cadenza's head,/ A tiny crippled heart was born" (ST, 12). These shifts are not the collaged, prose transitions of *The Tennis Court Oath*.

What intrudes most here is not the world of business and news-paper. The imagery is that of sexual trauma, and it is this trauma that is later developed into Ashbery's recurrent image of the dwarf and other regressive, passive *personae*.

In "The Instruction Manual" (ST, 14–18) the poet masterfully employs a long Whitmanesque line with an utterly plebeian tone. In his "Craft Interview" for the *New York Quarterly* (No. 9, Winter 1972), Ashbery speaks of "an expanded means of ut-terance . . . saying a very long thing in place of what might have originally been a much more concise one is an overflow of the meaning" (pp. 25–26). What is important to discriminate, however, is the early use of Whitman's long line for parodis-tically dry effects, and the later use of voluptuously imagistic sentences drawn on the analogy of Giorgio de Chirico's long paragraphs in *Hebdomeros*. The discursive theme of "The In-struction Manual" concerns a sensuous daydream and the ex-otic, as in Baudelaire's "L'Invitation au Voyage" or Hart Crane's opulent sea pieces. The poet is presenting in dramatistic terms the same theme adumbrated by Freud, namely "the relation of the poet to the daydreamer." The poet is presented as a drab worker, fantasizing a world of music and color and holiday. But the fantasy itself suffers from the banality of the worker and his *tedium vitae* has obviously affected the overtly touristlike attrac-tions discovered in Guadalajara. As in T. S. Eliot, "We have lingered in the chambers of the sea," but the poet wakes not because of any human voices but for the inhuman prose of the rational "Instruction Manual." "The Instruction Manual" also succeeds in its wonderful framing and poem-within-a poem de-vice, quite languorously a poem-within-a-manual-within-a-poem. The fantasy of Guadalajara is not presented with the forced passion of French surrealism but framed and informed always by *tedium vitae*. Even revolt is a modest thing.

"The Grapevine" (ST, 19) announces immediately its theme

of cognition somehow blurred through rhythmical abstractions that do not completely make sense: "Of who we and all they are/ You all now know. But you know/ After they began to find us out we grew." The personal pronouns and their comical melée remind one of Lewis Carroll and Gertrude Stein. What is indeed presented is a scheme in which cognitive processes, like Carroll's chess games, are choked in terms of paradoxical flux and stasis: "Whom must we get to know/ To die, so you live and we know?" Cognition here is a temptation.

These *unanswerable questions* are like the dream paradoxes of "A Boy" (ST, 20–21): *"It had been raining but/ It had not been raining."* It presents vividly what "The New Critics" had not fully investigated: the poetry of mental conflict, not simply irony and tension. Ashbery, like Hart Crane, is filled with the colorful factuality of contradictory feelings. The poetry is filled with the fears, monsters, phantasms, and particularly the castration-fears of childhood. The father is presented as a Jabberwocky, cloaked in strange vegetation: "Could the old man, face in the rainweed,/ Ask more smuttily?" (ST, 20). Again, the poem comments on its anomalous syntax indirectly *"He/ Couldn't lie.* He'd tell 'em by their syntax" (ST, 20). The boy's feelings of transparency and passivity are heightened by this admission in an otherwise dense and syntactically anomalous piece. Sexuality and history are confused richly in the last evocative pun: "The observer, the mincing flag. *An unendurable age"* (ST, 21).

"Glazunoviana" (ST, 22) is a truncated sonnet, with the initial expectation of an octet lopped by a line and the sestet equally dessicated. It is a dream catalogue of "nonsensical" questions: "The man with the red hat/ And the polar bear, is he here too?" (ST, 22). The second part contrasts with its grander declarations, including the demise of a bear and the advance of some "lovely tribes" to the north. The early dream landscapes of Ashbery are derived from Max Jacob, whose prose poems he translated extensively. Jacob and Picasso were much influenced by the *saltimbanques,* circus figures who appeared in the city as unusual types and absurdly isolated, archaic entertainers. All poets are archaistic now.

The early work of Ashbery is much concerned with this capturing of a melancholy aesthetic. Sudden sequels are like the sudden deaths of captured animals in zoos: "The bear/ Drops dead in sight of the window" (ST, 22). Always, the sense of heroism is diminished by comical adjectives, as in "The Hero" (ST, 23), a poem in trimeter couplets. Later, in his play "The Heroes,"[1] Ashbery was again to reduce the heroic to a more domestic scale. This truncating of the heroic, the puncturing of outmoded pieties, functions, in Freudian terms, to degrade the exalted. What is, however, redeemed, as in Waugh, Firbank, or Svevo, is a sense of more modest, modern manners amid camouflage: "like the first days/ Of good conduct" (ST, 23). Boyishness itself, as in the early Auden, a strong influence on Ashbery, is raised as a lyrical spectre in the face of dessicating adulthood with its sublimations and civilizations. Poetry is masterful regression.

Ashbery has frequently tried to redeem the archaic forms and in "Poem" (ST, 24–25) he employs the sestina without punctuation in a reminiscence of Apollinaire's "Zone." There is no attempt to recover the iambic of the classic sestina and one of the canonic rules concerning nouns as end-words is violated by the use of the end-verb "waiting." The theme itself is congruent with this incongruous syntax, for it is concerned with *unreality* or the feeling of the *uncanny:* "The road so strangely lit by lamps" (ST, 24). What might have been an easily Eliotic street of urban desolation is transformed by odd forebodings of the miraculous: "Peace to the fragrant hair/ Waiting for a tropical sky" (ST, 25).

The sestina gives the poet pushes in unexpected directions, and this sense of surrender to archaic forms is part of a more central sense of powerlessness. In "Album Leaf" (ST, 26) the diminished image of a bug is presented again in sudden death or possible survival: "If a bug fell from so high, would it land?" (ST, 26). The idea of mastery is raised in the quotation from Pasternak's *Safe Conduct*[2] used as epigraph to the parodic "The Picture of Little J.A. in a Prospect of Flowers": "He was spoilt from childhood by the future, which he mastered rather early and apparently without great difficulty" (ST, 27). Pasternak thought of Mayakovsky as a perfect analogue to the Revolution, but with some irony also pictured him as desperately requiring the opposition of the bourgeois philistine to have any energy.

Ashbery frames his past with all the careless artifice of a camera, but concludes each strophe with suddenly careful off-rhymes. He admits "this comic version" of himself is the only possible one he can redeem. Like the modest Pasternak, who finally exalted the quotidian in his doctor-poet Zhivago, the demotic, comic attitude is the only possible conversion. The rescue of the past lies in parody: "And only in the light of lost words/ Can we imagine our rewards" (ST, 29), and the task, as in Proust or Freud's *Psychopathology of Everyday Life*, is the redemption of what seems the most humble "slips of the tongue" and "accidents." Thus, the beggar, and diminished dream selves, combine to hint at a salvageable image of the poet rescued from the colorful traumas of childhood: "My head among the blazing phlox/ Seemed a pale and gigantic fungus" (ST, 28). This early poem was later to be celebrated by the painter Fairfield Porter in his address to a Guggenheim Museum audience (New York, 1972; unpublished) as a first sign that the poet was original, intrigued by the laws of contingency, and wiser in his uncertainties "than the assurances" of the tech-

nitas enjoyed formerly. The contemporary poet raises this
age of community only with an image of a lewd peaceable
ngdom:

> And oh beside the roaring
> Centurion of the lion's hunger
> Might not child and pervert
> Join hands, in the instant
> Of their interest, in the shadow
> Of a million boats; their hunger
> From loss grown merely a gesture?
>   (ST, 36)

The theme is not merely the fashionable "polymorphous perversity" of the child, or infantile sexuality in the Freudian sense
and its recovery by the adult; nor is the theme merely a parody
of the Greek community, now shown to be something slightly
curious in its permissions and pederasty. There is a lament for
the inconsequence of the modern poet and his sexualizing of the
exterior ("inserted in/ The panting forest" [ST, 35]). The possible landscape is one of surreal accommodation between lion, million boats, child, and pervert. The boats function as a kind of
image of the manufactured multiplicity in which the poet is
later to be disoriented in "They Dream Only of America" ("To
be lost among the thirteen million pillars of grass" [TCO, 13]).
His ambivalent recantation of such multiplicity is seen again in
"Chaos."

Ashbery not only uses the monotonies of repetition in his
poem "Canzone" (ST, 44–45), a form also loved by Auden, but
employs a blank tone for its flat dynamics. The flat style has
been praised by Ashbery as he finds it in Roussel, whose long
poems have been likened by Ashbery—in Roussel's favor—to
the prose of the Larousse dictionary. Just as Ashbery in his later
works employs the comically obtuse style of the popular novel,

nologists. Surely, the nostalgic evocations
rural scenery, opposed to the almost sickenin
camera, however enticing, was later to le
Wordsworthian evocations in *The Double Drea*

In Ashbery's work, repetition of words, place
devices (as in the off-rhymed couplets of "The Pi
J.A.") take an alarmingly large place. The archaic
pantoum, employed originally in Malaya, and use
Hugo and Charles Baudelaire, appealed to Ashber
dreamlike and powerful repetition of whole lines.
lairean synaesthesia is employed throughout: "Thro
vague snow of many clay pipes," and a Stevens-like
"Yes, sirs, connoisseurs of oblivion" (ST, 30). Synaesthes
longed-for wholeness of the sensations.

"Grand Abacus" (ST, 32–33) again uses the long W
manesque lines for businesslike purposes: "its commercial a
etiolated visage" (ST, 32). There is, however, a presentation
childhood with its nightmares and fantasies. Monster imagery is
presented with false naiveté: "The skin is perhaps children, they
say, 'We children. . . .' " The theme of transformations, peculiarly abrupt metamorphoses, is used portentously. A simple de-
nouement makes the closure all the more horrifying: " 'We do
not want to fly away.' But it is already too late. The children
have vanished" (ST, 33).

"The Mythological Poet" treats the same theme that W. H.
Auden raised in his foreword to *Some Trees:* the idiosyncratic
and private imagery of the modern poet opposed to the canonic
mythos of antiquity's poet. The poems of Ashbery celebrate (as
in the poem "Chaos" [ST, 38–39]) the true inconsequences of
contemporary nightmare, and one might construct an entirely
historical context in which to frame Ashbery's poetry of urban
negativity. The poet is forced to admire in nostalgia the *com-*

and in *Three Poems* parodies the flourishing pieties of religious bombast, so in "Canzone" he attempts to gain the two-dimensionality sought by Robbe-Grillet and Saurraute in their "new" novels. A classic target for parody is the very pretentious academic, and Ashbery too likes to take on pretentious decorative forms, not only of academics, but of *litterateurs* in general, and create through these oddly jerking, archaic forms his theme of *the new* and *the uncanny:* "odd lights can/ Fall on sinking clay" (ST, 46).

This early book explicitly states (like Koch's poem on "misunderstandings" entitled "Taking a Walk with You,"[3]) the subject of the psychopathology of everyday life, its nonsense "errors," remarked about in the anomalous syntax: "What flower tolling on the waters/ You stupefied me" (ST, 47). Already, despite the more normal tetrameters in the poem "Errors," we see the poet leading to his later disjunctive style in which copulas are abandoned and ideas presented in shocking simultaneity. Ashbery's poetry is a carnival of disconnection. "Only disconnect," says the Menippean satirist.

"Illustration" (ST, 48–50) is one of Ashbery's most extended poems concerning suicide. It suffers perhaps from being a bit too explicit, and the diction is still very obviously influenced by Wallace Stevens:

> A novice was sitting on a cornice
> High over the city. Angels
>
> Combined their prayers with those
> Of the police, begging her to come off of it.
> (ST, 48)

The Suicide is seen as an aestheticization of the ethical, as in Kierkegaard: "Much that is beautiful must be discarded/ So that we may resemble a taller/ Impression of ourselves" (ST, 49).

The discarding, the selectivities of the poet, later to become the familiar "leaving-out business" of "The Skaters" (RAM, 39), are here likened to the suicide itself. The community is comically defeated in its attempt to pierce the aesthetic armor of the "novice," who seems a poet, both in her wishes ("I desire/ Monuments" [ST, 48]) and also in the insecurity of her position and idiosyncrasy of her relations. The poet comments, as *an illustration*, that the "Moths climb in the flame,/ Alas, that wish only to be the flame" (ST, 49), wittily mocking Rimbaud's notion of the poet turning himself into a seer of chaos. The lucidity of suicide is likened to the lucidity of artful ceremony: "effigy/ Of indifference, a miracle/ Not meant for us, as the leaves are not/ Winter's because it is the end" (ST, 50). The isolation of the "novice" is seen as final in an ending reminiscent of Stevens' "The Course of a Particular" or "The Snow Man"[4] where the misery of a final drift toward nothingness seems to be the only possible theme, undecorated finally and all the more disturbing. Such poetry questions solipsism as relentlessly as any analytic philosophy.

Ashbery's poem "Some Trees" (ST, 51) is an anthology piece but has never been adequately analyzed. It is more than a charming dream landscape in five rhyming couplets, with many interesting assonances and off-rhymes. It is also one of the central and abiding poetic illusions concerning *randomness* and *dream logic*, by the poet. While the religious theme in Ashbery is usually one of despair, and piety usually parodied, contingency itself is praised as decoratively as possible. "Some Trees" does not lament but celebrates the "noise" of modern life, like the "prepared piano" in the work of John Cage (who influenced the collage pieces of Ashbery's middle works [interview]). This little poem attempts to appraise and praise "the pleasant surprises" of the amazing if quotidian trees in their chance arrangements. Randomness is not seen merely against the order of metrics (trimeter and tetrameter) or a rhyme scheme, but as part of the unpolished contingency of things themselves, which the poet prefers to more orderly spectacles and narratives. The trees are not melodramatic, excessive: "as though speech/ Were a still performance/ Arranging by chance/ . . . their merely being there/ Means something; that soon/ We may touch, love, explain" (ST, 51). The poet alludes to *an explanation*, a padding *by significance* he eschews in his later work; here it stands for the possible sexualizing connection that the arrangement of "some trees" suggests. The poet "is surrounded" but not with any defeated passivity. Malice and self-laceration are overcome by the lyricism of "Such comeliness . . ./ A canvas on which emerges// A chorus of smiles" (ST, 51).

The self collapses in most of Ashbery's poems, and dialogues too may collapse, as in the broken love affairs of the late *Three Poems*, but here there is a hint of otherness not viewed as threatening. Concealment is a theme, but here it is more proportionately sought as "reticence": "Our days put on such reticence/ These accents seem their own defense" (ST, 51). The "puzzling light" of this canvas is part of the world of uncertainty and confusion that is seen as sexually, visually, and mentally viable: a reticence of self-aware ignorance. The trees and the inscape are seen as adaptable, not merely as binary oppositions. The poet of "Some Trees" and "Le Livre est sur la table" (ST, 74–75)—another early masterpiece—does not need the ornamental or the *too surprising* within every line. There is here a sense of simplicity, as in Gertrude Stein, and the summaries ("All beauty, resonance, integrity" [ST, 74]) are not merely false summations, or false logic as in Jorge Luis Borges. Ashbery loves the false scholarship of Borges, and particularly his crypto-scholarly catalogues, but in the early poems summary is used to allude to the Shakespearean chord of "The Phoenix and the Turtle," a species of love poem and *threnos* based on the horror of *Fortuna* and contingency. At a time when Robert Rauschenberg, John Cage, and Merce Cunningham were experimenting with popular culture and the dance of indeterminacy, Ashbery also investigated the linguistic possibilities of these elements. As it happens, language is already the indeterminate dance *par excellence*. In "Some Trees" he celebrates rural contingency and uses a decorous diction, derived from Stevens, to speak of the more reticent of chance arrangements.

In "Some Trees" the poet performs his most graceful enjambments. These enjambments tend to remind one of a false luxury, a faded elegance now being deposed. There is a surrounding of the seemingly spurious (noise, puzzling light, reticence, defense), but these qualities are finally redeemed. The "feminine" rhyme of "morning" and "agreeing" is used to contrast with the simple and more sudden textures of "I" and "try." Dissonant off-rhymes are used, such as "there" and "are," "soon" and "explain," and these purposely blunted rhymes finally capitulate to a cadence and classical rhyme in closure, with its graceful *regularity:* "Our days put on such reticence/ These accents seem their own defense" (ST, 51). Rhyme and metrics too may be regarded as a species of camouflage in Ashbery, an older costume handed to the poet by the tradition and handled gracefully. Rhymes, too, are associated in "Some Trees" with the complex pastoral, as later in "Ella Wheeler Wilcox" (DDS, 24). The nuances of these early metrics are opposed to the seamless prose of the degraded stories of popular culture, such as "Idaho" (TCO, 91). Strophe, metrics, and rhyme are part of the poetics of landscape and love gratified, rather than of the poetics of despair and *camp*.

"The Painter" (ST, 54–55) is a witty sestina investigating the development of a contemporary artist, here figured as painter, up to the extreme moment of "leaving the canvas/ Perfectly white" (ST, 55). One is reminded of Robert Rauschenberg's white canvasses of the 1950s and of his famous "Erased de Kooning." Ashbery is also involved in the possibility of *leaving things alone:* "That nature, not art, might usurp the canvas?" (ST, 54). Here Ashbery uses the comic repetitions of the sestina and tetrameters ("Sitting between the sea and the buildings") and many flat quotidian nouns, as influenced by Elizabeth Bishop's sestinas: *buildings, portrait, prayer, subject, brush, canvas.* The audience is seen as part of an urban mob that denounces the aesthete and tosses him the portrait "from the tallest of the buildings" (ST, 55). Here is an apt artistic defeat, not like that of "Illustration," where the suicide has been aesthetisized, but a victory for the funny philistinism of the poet's audience, philistine nature itself: "And the sea devoured the canvas and the brush."

A more nostalgic work is the poem "And You Know" (ST, 56–59) in which the poet uses what seems an acceptable discursiveness within a Whitmanesque exposition of childhood. Suddenly, however, the narrative is vitiated or at least dramatically twisted by dreamlike *non sequiturs:* "We fly to the nearest star, whether it be red like a furnace, or yellow" (ST, 58). The authority of teachers develops into the portentous theme of an aging into meaninglessness and a tedious drifting into dreams. This drifting is also a refusal: "Goodbye, my master and my dame" (ST, 58), and also a voyage from this early, insidious nostalgia itself: "And the night, the endless, muggy night that is invading our school" (ST, 59).

In "Meditations of a Parrot" (ST, 63) (rather than "Meditations upon a Parrot") Ashbery gives a truly Morgensternesque nonsense song. The *appoggiaturas* in the poem remind one of Stevens' "Bantams in Pine-Woods" (*The Collected Poems,* p. 75). The use of alliteration for comic effect is pronounced: "All *sweetly st*ood up the *s*ea to me" (ST, 63). And color too is used to capture the sea in a more domesticated mood, "Like blue cornflakes in a white bowl" (ST, 63). Here Marvell's "green thoughts in a green shade" seem alluded to and mocked. The whole poem proceeds by *non sequitur:* "The girl said, 'Watch this.'/ I come from Spain, I said./ I was purchased at a fair./ She said, 'None of us know' " (ST, 63). Like the poem entitled "A Long Novel" (ST, 64–65), which is really a short poem, these early meditations are everything *but* meditations. They are really the songlike ejaculations of the poet who "parrots" his poetry in a modern *mimesis* of discontinuity afforded to him by the tradition of Rimbaud and Corbière's songs. The most successful examples of this fabulous poetry of *non sequitur* is seen in "Answering a Question in the Mountains" and "Le Livre est sur la table," which conclude *Some Trees.*

In "Answering a Question in the Mountains" (ST, 70–71) Rimbaldien imagery of illumination and *ekstasis* predominates:

> I went into the mountains to interest myself
> In the fabulous dinners of hosts distant and demure.
>
> The foxes followed with endless lights.
>
> (ST, 70)

But the poet's expectations of mastery are presented in terms both domestic and austere: "Some day I am to build the wall/ Of the box in which all angles are shown" (ST, 70). This mathematical image seems both to allude to the *arcana* of the Kabbala and the playroom of the infantile.

The bizarre grammar is used *precisely* and not simply for the dazzlements of inconsequence: "It is late to be late" (ST, 70). In the second part of "Answering a Question in the Mountains" the poet uses not only uncanny syntax ("Let us ascend trees in our heads,/ The dull heads of trees" [ST, 70]) but an unexpectedly glamorous Stevensesque image of fragrance and peacock perfection ("The perfumed toque of dawn" [ST, 71]) and yet immediately contrasts this with the dull texture of night ("The hysteric evening with empty hands" [ST, 71]). Like Ezra Pound, Ashbery is capable of great cinematic compression, and here he uses montage to great effect: "The snow creeps by; many light years pass" (ST, 71). This rhythm is later to recur in a lyrical passage in "The Skaters": "The west wind grazes my cheek, the droplets come pattering down" (RAM, 54). But Ashbery makes fabulous prophecy out of a lesson of grammar:

> We see for the first time.
> We shall see for the first time.
> We have seen for the first time.
> (ST, 71)

This is surely what Jakobson means by "the poetry of grammar." The poem gives, in this short space, an entirely immediate experience of perception, subtly framed, and a little essay on language itself. Grammar is made to be the subject of the poem, and at the same time points to its necessary connections with *all perception*. The poem, however, concludes on a more or less demure or fastidious note:

> I cannot agree or seek
> Since I departed in the laugh of diamonds
> The hosts of my young days.
> (ST, 71)

Thus Ashbery gives us his little glamorous illumination, and then his modest reappraisal of its enthusiastic boyishness of tone.

"Le Livre est sur la table" (ST, 74–75) is one of Ashbery's most exquisite works upon the concept of chastity and rarity, both aesthetic and ethical. It begins with a summation that beauty exists by its idiosyncratic position or by its very absence. In tercets resembling Wallace Stevens', we are presented with a woman walking by an ocean and with a sensuality conceived by the poet in all plenitude. But the first part ends with sudden portentous questions of wretchedness and misery:

> . . . But what
>
> Dismal scene is this? the old man pouting
> At a black cloud, the woman gone
> Into the house, from which the wailing starts?
> (ST, 74)

A great deal of the poem concerns the possibility, as in "The Painter," of nature rescuing the artist by its own effects. Man is presented as humbly placing a birdhouse as a species of sculpture on the shore. But the sea itself is an author: "the sea/ Which goes on writing" (ST, 75). It is the line-drawing of the sea, eternally written and also self-effacing, to which the poet aspires. Here is a most sensuous image of Ashbery's ideals of *aesthesis*. Though he has said in interviews that the visual does not concern him, his metaphor here is the meaningless "line-drawing" that the waves make upon the beach. These grooves of nature seem to be worshipped by "the gods," and in their senseless way take on some of the curves of the woman. But the poem ends in unanswered questions concerning this "automatic writing":

> . . . Is the bird mentioned
> In the waves' minutes, or did the land advance?
> (ST, 75)

The poem's question is a poignant reminder of the possible final erasure of all art, man-made or ready-made or natural. This is the extreme beauty which exists "by deprivation," and we comprehend this beauty through our incomprehensions: "Walks and wears her hair and knows/ All that she does not know" (ST, 74). Our phantasmagorical cognition is our only plentitude:

> . . . Yet we know
>
> What her breasts are. And we give fullness
> To the dream.
>
> (ST, 74)

While the diction has still the glamorous values of early Wallace Stevens, and the landscape seems grandly primary and vivid, Ashbery pursues in "Le Livre est sur la table" most diligently his theme of form from fertile formlessness. While the land may advance to devour the poetry of the waves, the hermetic secrets of the sand remain, like the submerged impulses of our "buried lives." For Ashbery, early and late, the image of effacement, and particularly self-effacement, is paradoxically redeemed by its *eventful* nature, the continuity of its discontinuity: "in the shadow of the sea/ Which goes on writing" (ST, 75). This is, at once, a poem most humorous and grave.

Thus, Ashbery concluded his earliest manner: recurrent dream imagery, exquisite modulations, archaistic formal devices, Whitmanesque parodies, grammatical anomalies. His scale still lacks the epic cohesions of the later "Europe," "The Skaters," and, most importantly, the three prose meditations. In the early work, a delicate, Mozartian tone is most consistently struck, and the darker problems of masochism explored in exquisite miniature: "I placed flowers on your path/ Because I wanted to be near you./ Do not punish me."[5]

While abstract expressionists were constantly discussing, from 1940 to 1960, problems of gigantism of scale, Ashbery remains intimist in his early works. These are touching minutiae of dreams and scenes of dislocated seduction and enchantment. Vivid color is already used to give a final funny sense of awkward identity, and the insecure early poet eschews any vatic role. What is not enucleated is the grand desiccation of the later collages, the labyrinthine mania of "The Skaters," and the possible conversions lapsed in the major prose pieces. But in his early syntheses of Stein, Stevens, and French surrealism, Ashbery demonstrates utter finesse. Never again is limpidity employed so continuously concerning the themes of discontinuity and opacity.

CHAPTER 3

The Period of Collage: The Tennis Court Oath

Ashbery's early period ends with a synthesis of glamorous diction and erotic-aesthetic dislocations in the French surrealist mode. In his next period, a new prosiness intrudes. Discursiveness is dislocated, but most often by the drab tones of cheap literature and newspaperese. Haunting dreams and nightmares are contrasted most consistently with the bleak world of business and metropolis. The usual bejewelled landscapes are exchanged for machine imagery. Masques and rituals are presented only briefly, in a few archaistic sonnets and formulaic pieces, and most often a horrid daylight world reigns. Serious play has begun.

While smaller poems are presented, this period is the first to include many poems of great duration and scope. These poems of scale, like "Europe," "America," "Idaho," are, on the other hand, built up by extremely fractured images, uncannily flat jumbles of *non sequiturs* which Ashbery somehow manages to control. The flatness produces a new sensation of the extremely humiliating and reifying aspects of modern life. Songlike passages, reminiscent of the early style, intrude but usually serve only to underline the evocation of horror. "Wit" is employed throughout, but it too is usually directed against the *personae* of the collages. And the *personae* themselves begin to become extremely vapid and dissociated. These collage poems function as a mature collapse into the everyday, and they oppose the simpler dream techniques of the early Ashbery.

The Tennis Court Oath is a book which stands at the center of Ashbery's *collagiste* period. Its first poem, "The Tennis Court Oath" (TCO, 11–12) was inspired by the humorous statues of Louis David's heroic "Tennis Court Oath" picture, which represents the proponents of that precursor of the Revolution in a most gallant moment.[1] Unfortunately, or fortunately for Ashbery's figure of irony, the personages in the Louis David picture have never been fully painted, and remain, in the sketch, in the nude. This nudity, however, does not vitiate the very fully dressed nature of their smug classic gestures and posings, and the whole effect is thus a typical dreamlike embarrassment: To be caught with one's pants down, while initiating a great revolution with one's peers. The situation has all the typical traits of an Ashbery joke: the whole precisely rendered, and yet somehow, and vitally, incomplete; the whole ceremonious and public, and yet vitiated by the unnerving privacy that cannot be concealed; the neoclassic wit punctuated by utter modern nakedness; and finally, Ashbery's use of the "title" alone of this event, with no mention of Louis David, or the reasons behind his selection. And yet even in the case of the Louis David painting alone (I leave aside for the moment the poem), the transformation is paradigmatically Ashberyan, since it was achieved by *contingency* alone, the accident of the painter's not finishing the canvas. Time finishes us and/or leaves us unfinished.

In the poem, throughout, there is a central sense of incompletion; almost every sentence reads as a possible fragment, syntactically desiccated. There is also a sense of portentous punctuation by death: "there is a terrible breath," "I worry," "The doctor and Philip had come over the road/ . . . your fears were justified/ the blood shifted . . ./ the patient finished" (TCO, 11–12). In this opening poem, Ashbery has achieved a great transition, in many senses, from his early work, *Some Trees, Turandot*, and *The Poems*. The diction is no longer Stevensian in any sense; it has suddenly achieved the tone and often *the look of shattered newsprint*, as in Pop paintings of this period (1956–1962). It has a flat prose quality which is the first, severe initiation for the reader into this period in Ashbery: "horse strains fatigued I guess . . . the calls" (TCO, 11). The other aspect of this middle style may be seen in the way the automatic imagery of the first books has now dissolved even further, so that even within lines a few utterly isolated configurations may jostle and juxtapose. This severe juxtaposition leads Ashbery, in the final apotheosis of the cubist derangement, "Europe" (TCO, 64–85), to isolate dangling clauses and words alone. "The Tennis Court Oath" does seem to have a fractured narrative, as in the later prose poem "Idaho" (TCO, 91), perhaps a narrative "lifted" from one of the cheap novels Ashbery often uses for his materials, "taken from the quays of Paris," as it were, homely material that might include a sentence like "The doctor and Philip had come over the road" (TCO, 11). Ashbery does not write "naturally" in that way: this is a parody and homage to one fashionable prose style, a "cheap" or "degraded" prose style. "The Tennis Court Oath" is more than interlaced with snippets; in fact, it is difficult to tell where these collage pieces leave off or start.

One of the curious effects of this transformation of "The Tennis Court Oath" into complete and seamless *collage* is the curtailing of the "I" as having much lyric or dramatic nuance. The "I" may now merely be the "I" *not of a persona* but of a piece of *newspaperese* or newspaper, or part of a story pasted, as it were, upon the poem. There is no more of Ashbery to this "I" than the "I" of an alien bit of prose from another source shockingly "fallen into" the poem. The "I" is, indeed, often necessarily linked to the continuous "ego" or "je" of the poem, but a radical deflation of its resonance or dignity has occurred. As a matter of fact, Ashbery in this period employs the various kinds of "I" much in the way more conventional masks are employed by Yeats or Eliot, but in Ashbery's extreme case there is only the bitter sense of the two-dimensionality of the collaged "I." This is his "schizo-analysis."

It is necessary to dwell on this radical flattening out of the *persona*. Perhaps one of the most dramatic and chilling effects of the middle period is the *very lack of conventional drama* that Ashbery commands: a modulation into the inhuman, where the lyric voice ends and merely manufactured objects remain. Jasper Johns' art, meditated upon by Ashbery in his years as art critic, is illuminating here. Johns chose in the 1950s and 1960s purposely to work with given objects: a flag, a target, sets of numbers, beer cans, maps, and numerals. Ashbery has revealed in conversation his sympathies for this art. And his own art at this time often manipulates, *through collage,* the given and manipulates the element of the "I" impersonally and often seemingly in random fashion, though always with his "signature." There can be no "utter" randomness to this manipulation. Manipulation always assumes predilections and taste, if only the taste for what is to be abandoned: the naturalistic "I."

The impression of many of these poems is of *trompe-l'oeil* and a quality of *the given*. It leaves one often feeling that nothing indeed has been tampered with or manipulated; in short, that there is "no art," because the artifice has been in the selection and juxtaposition of given elements. In Ashbery's case however extreme tact and solicitude have been employed for the incandescence from juxtaposition, and this is what shocks in his middle collages.

"They Dream Only Of America" is one of the most horrifying of Ashbery's middle period poems. It begins explicitly with dream imagery, and proceeds to an image, in psychoanalytic jargon, of *identity loss* and confusion, which is grim indeed: "To be lost among the thirteen million pillars of grass" (TCO, 13). This is followed by a couplet in idiosyncratic isolation, in quotation marks, though not for any specifiable reason, except for the reason of their isolated decorativeness: " 'This honey is delicious/ *Though it burns the throat*' " (TCO, 13). Actually, the quotation marks initiate a vague sense that a dialogue is being created or overheard, or that the poem itself is a monologue in various strata, and that when the writer wishes to modulate his voice, he has merely to use the inverted commas to achieve an effect of isolation, of entering a new level of the dream. The poem follows with an interesting and characteristic conflation of detective story prose and comment on childhood: "And hiding from darkness in barns/ They can be grownups now/ And the murderer's ash tray is more easily" (TCO, 13). But this is followed by a dramatic dash and the enigmatic statement: "The lake a lilac cube" (TCO, 13). Now it is an extraordinarily chilling fact that this statement is both a sudden glimpse of a lake and a garden, and also a kind of noise or static used to cover up the detective story mystery. Just as certain false clues are distributed in detective stories, so the Ashbery poem abounds in certain false clues and hints—producing percussive "effects." Landscape is here used, for example, as a shifting away from the menacing detective scene. The lake thus becomes all the more dramatically serene.

The next stanza ("He holds a key in his right hand" [TCO, 13]) is a stanza of pathos in which the ubiquitous Ashbery fig-

ure, like Henri Michaux's Plume, arrives in all powerlessness.
Then follows another discursive, seemingly sensible passage
about driving. Car imagery in Ashbery usually conjures up
night and mystery, a ride into trauma and through time and its
horror. The car is a species of gliding animal within his poems,
and heavily eroticized. The car drives "through dandelions"
(TCO, 13). One accepts these strange dandelions because one is
within a fairytale landscape, and because this part of the poem,
as any path in Russian folklore, is the most inviting.
Then follows a kind of parody of detective stories: "Was the
cigar a sign?/ And what about the key?" (TCO, 13). In this poem
the poet is humiliating one's usual expectations for significance,
as he is to do time and time again in "The Skaters" when he refuses to stuff his poems with explanatory material (RAM, 39).
The last stanza is a final and dismal paradox: "There is nothing
to do/ For our liberation, except wait in the horror of it" (TCO,
13). Ashbery here gives his ironic horror of waking up, of unravelling the false clues, of too lucidly liberating the self from
daydream and daymare, from fantasy and art. Ashbery ends this
"dream" poem with a lyric coda, put in quotation marks, so as
not to place too clearly this speech in the mouth of the Poet
alone: "And I am lost without you" (TCO, 13). This final bit of
apostrophizing seems to be a too neat closure of the poem, except that the piece ends with the "you" undefined (America?
beloved?) and the "I" even more strenuously the unresolved "I"
of the middle period collages.

"Thoughts of a Young Girl" is a kind of truncated, free sonnet: a rhyme scheme of a certain awkwardness is evolved,
ABABCD, that trails off into the almost unrhymed sestet,
EFGAHI.[2] In a way, this poem would not seem so neat if it
were not for the fact that a strong pentameter rules it: "It is
such a beautiful day I had to write you a letter," "And drowned
in the bathtub of the world," "And now I let you go. Signed,

The Dwarf" (TCO, 14). With less betrayals of the norm than is usual in Ashbery's middle poems, it is also a sparkling foretaste of the neoclassic wit of the parodic sections of "The Skaters." The poem has typical "Pop" imagery of the quotidian: "the bathtub of the world," and deals with the meek, ever-defeated, ever-resilient fool that haunts Ashbery's poems. This fool, with Charlie Chaplin as a celebrated precursor, does seem to stand here perhaps unambiguously as the "je" of the poem. On the other hand, it is equally possible for this dwarf to be *the girl* of the poem, and for the first part of the poem to be the document, the letter, written to the stronger "I" of the last part. The "Dwarf" of the first passage would then be transformed to the sphinx of the sestet: "And the smile still played about her lips/ As it has for centuries" (TCO, 14). One of the more delightful juxtapositions (and this is one of the more cavalier love poems in Ashbery's *oeuvre*) is the last apostrophe: "Oh my daughter,/ My sweetheart, daughter of my late employer, princess,/ May you not be long on the way!" (TCO, 14). This poem, in *The Tennis Court Oath*, with all its charm, sonnetlike logic, and uneasy comprehensibility, its limpid facility, is ominously and immediately followed by the immensely bleak collage poem entitled "America" (TCO, 15).

"America," like the last poem in the collection, "Europe," is paradoxically both hermetic and public, and is based on a series of endless dénouements or isolations of words. These concatenations or aggregates of words build up a tone of "Lament" in an almost German-expressionist sense of that word. "Piling upward/ the fact the stars" (TCO, 15). These piled-up stars and facts are actually a bitter reminder of the dreary accumulation of "given" or "fact" in the fetishes of America itself. The poem is a lament with *no persona;* it is merely a presentation, in a purely symbolic art of sensuous illusion, of the sensuousness and lack of it in the spectacle of mass society. "We were parked/ Millions of us/ The accident was terrible" (TCO, 15). Punctuation itself is here used as a quality of poetry's graphesis, another abstract-expressionist "drip" in a canvas of contingencies. One can no longer ascribe even the punctuation or lack of it to the systematic hand of the author; the punctuation now seems to come merely out of the bleak air of the public system of collage itself. The punctuation in Stein and Cummings was at least to some extent a systematic shorthand on the part of the authors: one could create with it a floating poetical sense. Here, Ashbery presents us with elements which seem to be snipped from another reality, that of newspapers, detective stories, and perhaps older poems and other literary forms. At times, too, the collage seems suspended and the author or *skena* faintly intrudes, but again in severely truncated manner: "Ribbons/ over the Pacific" (TCO, 15).

What one must decide after locating this collagiste and "given" quality of the Ashbery lines is how well, how *dramatically*, the author has made his modulations: Does the poem retain dramatic tension, maturity, structure? This Leavisite question is one not easily answered, since the novelty of the poem is so overwhelming. The criteria for structures, poetical and other, are seemingly exploded by the collage, in the sense that collages *assume* and advance new criteria. Just so the plasticity or the *facture* of Renaissance painting could no longer be held as a central value within flatter abstractions. Ashbery's topic of exhaustion, for example, demands a drab drama.

Let us define, then, what we think are the successes in structure and rhythm of this Ashbery poem. First, there is the successfully *flat* juxtaposition that escapes the merely concrete and demotic of W. C. Williams and creates a trancelike minimalism ("The pear tree/ moving me" [TCO, 15]), what one might call a shorthand and what is now a new *collage-imagism*, concrete dictions, suspended in the colloid of the largely abstract. Ashbery's modulation of tone, too, is dramatic: it is not merely quick, not merely speedy mid-career tergiversations. There are long passages in which the modulation is very subtle: "The pear tree/ moving me/ I am around   and in my sigh/ The gift of a the stars./ The person/ Horror—the morsels of his choice" (TCO, 15). Here one sees Ashbery's gift for sustaining a grey impressionism with a simple diction, neither tainted by his early Stevensiana, nor leaning utterly to the drab. Instead of metrics, one has a continual and successfully stressed line, as in W. C. Williams, but always ending in cadences guaranteed not to insure an organic sense, as of breath, but the inorganic dead sense of collaged material from a lively if indifferent universe. The little lyric moments ("You girl/ the sea in waves" [TCO, 17]) seem like brief remittances from Ashbery's early works in a poem so newly fragmented, so forbidding. The successful end is another instance of this momentary cohesion: "A feather not snow blew against the window./ A signal from the great outside" (TCO, 19). The most central, then, of Ashbery's middle-period criteria for structural success is in distribution of the elements of discontinuity so that they are just held in balance, or framed, by the fewest necessary cohesive elements.

Elements of continuity may be *simple tone*, or may be a similar simple *set* of images: in "America," the public imagery, in "Europe," the plane imagery, in the later "The Skaters," imagery of art, voyage, and solitude. While structurally the poems may vacillate, the Proust-like repetition of the elements never in a sense guarantees more than a vague impression of narrative, never rises toward the dangerous omen of a plot but gives *a taste of a plot*. Nevertheless, this element of parsimoniously repetitious imagery or sheer musical repeat ("The Skaters" simply repeating the central motif of the skaters, or "The New Spirit" continuing again and again the motif of conversion) is what the author once called "the subject matter of poetry—the way things happen."[3] Like Valéry, Ashbery has mastered monotony and made it moan.

Ashbery's middle collages, with neutral, colorless subject-matter, are not dictated by the mere discursive or denotative demands of the signifiers; the words ("his happy stance/ position   peace/ on earth/ ignited fluid/ before he falls" [TCO, 19]) are indeed to be scrutinized and used for all their denotativeness, but the shredded quality of these isolate signifiers impedes the usual rapport with the signified. In depriving portion after portion of these middle period poems of a narrative or a conventional referentiality, Ashbery asserts the collapse of such mimetic conventions as an active theme. This is a negative statement of his concerns; but largely his poetry is one of *via negativa*, and suffers most when it lacks all of this frozen fullness and seems merely, as in some early work, precious or tame.

Throughout *The Tennis Court Oath* older forms are used only mockingly, as if to remind one of their former uses as images of order, stasis, conventional public health, and security of status and values. The poems "Dido" and "The Idiot," called "Two Sonnets," are explicitly in their titles images of the rejected and the refused as they are ennobled through lucid lament. The poem concerning Dido is a comprehensible if archaistic statement concerning self-love and self-pollution interwoven much in the way Yeats' palace of Love and excrement were congruent: "The body's products become/ Fatal to it. Our spit/ Would kill us, but we/ Die of our heat" (TCO, 20). The first sonnet cheats the sonnet itself of perfection, as Aeneas cheated Dido of completion. Ashbery's work uses this image of the spurned lover systematically as his image of disorder and frustration. Discontinuity within human relationships, as in Eliot's mechanical love seductions and relationships, is paradigmatic of a world in which manufactured objects reign over humorless landscapes which the poet alone makes scenically "humorous": "The iodine bottle sat in the hall" (TCO, 20).

The sonnet "The Idiot" contains a conventional *Lament:* "I've wandered the wide world over./ No man I've known, no friendly beast/ Has come and put its nose into my hands" (TCO, 20). And it ends with a sestet reminiscent of "The Sheep" by W. H. Davies in its Georgian, or mock-Georgian pathos. The idiot, struggling with mariners to keep the boat from sinking, finds the waves of the unlucky storm congenial. The congeniality, the friendly disorder makes of Ashbery a true "connoisseur," not of chaos but of his own "oblivion," and to couch this oblivion in supposed "sonnet" form while retaining almost nothing of the conventional framework of the sonnet is his masterpiece of imperfection. To this pluralist, perfection is an imperfect idea.

The title of "To Redouté" (TCO, 21) refers to a painter known as "The Rembrandt of the Rose," and the poem is one of the most tender of Ashbery's "middle" period lyrics, looking backward in a sense to the more Stevens-like and even florid passages of the early verse and yet also looking forward to the Wordsworthian and pastoral quietism of the poems in *The Double Dream of Spring.* The poem begins with some marvelous evocations of impressionism's merged subject and object: "To true roses uplifted on the bilious tide of evening" (TCO, 21). It is filled with evocation of the haunting past, the usual early motif of dream and obsession: "My first is a haunting face/ In the hanging-down hair./ My second is water:/ I am a sieve" (TCO, 21). The second stanza introduces Ashbery's usual motif of novelty and aesthetic adventure, but in a new and disintegrating light: "My only new thing:/ The penalty of light forever" (TCO, 21). This poem reminds us, with its colors and objects ("The oval shape responds" . . . "Once approved the magenta must continue" [TCO, 21]) of the influence in Ashbery's life of his own art criticism and the art criticism associated with abstract expressionism and, also, of course, the painting around him. The final moment in "To Redouté" reminds us of "To the One of Fictive Music" of Stevens, particularly Stevens' last line ("The imagination that we spurned and crave" [4]) except that in Ashbery's case art itself, or the imagination, seems to be *lamenting* its own activity: "It grieves for what it gives:/ Tears that streak the dusty firmament" (TCO, 21). The difficulty with Ashbery's poem is the ambiguity of "the oval shape," but it is surely meant to be *the artifact* as much as Stevens' ambiguous "jar"—for Ashbery's poetry is filled with these brief hints as to the activity of art and its fetishes. The making of the poem, as in Stevens, is certainly, even as so briefly hinted in "To Redouté," one of the central themes of his "action poetry" and becomes the obsessive later theme of "The Skaters." Poetry traces itself before speaking, almost. Ashbery has little to learn now or later from Derrida.

In *The Tennis Court Oath*, there are many poems in which Ashbery attempts to sustain for some duration his new "collage" technique, with varying successes. "Night" (TCO, 22–24) has explicitly a dreamy and despairing theme ("The evening I offer you the easy aspirin of death" [TCO, 22]) but has some of its most horrifying effects in its flatness, a flatness that Ashbery had already studied in the prose and poetry of Roussel, whose art was flat as a micro-reduced dictionary. Not only is there colloquial imagery in juxtaposition with grander words ("the easy aspirin of death") but a use of the most awkward diction ("smelled the smell of") purposely to get a demotic quality of *stupor mundi* in the poetry. Just as Frank O'Hara used overheard conversation in his poetry, and as once James Joyce while dictating to Samuel Beckett permitted some overheard conversation hastily transcribed to remain, so Ashbery tends to try to embody this almost disembodied conversational style, in which snippets of the conversation are used for extreme ironic effects, effects which can be called "percussive" in the context of a noisy "modernism" in poetry. The poem returns to childhood reminiscence, filled with ellipses the better to indicate a nostalgic monologue. One stanza simply deliquesces to "Uh huh." A long series of dots seems to indicate greater and greater expunging, as in "The sad trash newspapers schedule complaint/ To belong to me.................." (TCO, 23). A typical Ashbery metaphor, derived from domestic images of Pasternak, is his colloquial "I guess the darkness stubbed its toe" (TCO, 24). The poem's last stanza is closer to a traditional tighter unit, with a sense of vanishing or "narrowing of space," but with a suddenness here as in the spoken end of traditional ballads: "The kids came and we all went the briars" (TCO, 24). The ending of "Night" reminds one of the speech-song device in music that was to influence Ashbery's poetry, the alternations between melody and spoken voice employed, for example, by the Viennese composer Arnold Schoenberg, the teacher of John Cage.

"How Much Longer Will I Be Able to Inhabit the Divine Sepulcher . . ." (TCO, 25-27) is a long, Prufrockian poem, one of the most traditional, the most Eliotic, of Ashbery's poems. It is also a strange specimen case of the best of his middle style collages showing the use of a more sustained *persona*. The "I" in this poem begins by asking questions in a lugubrious literary style, derived from a parodied Hölderlin (Hölderlin is Ashbery's favorite elegiac master). This is followed by the extraordinarily undercutting, percussive "Huh." More questions follow, concerning the other questions, but in most tangential ways. Still the basic denotation of the question, *what are we to understand concerning mortalia,* is plain. What follows is a slightly concealed stanza, concerning a mysterious "he" ("In pilgrim times he wounded me" [TCO, 25]) who seems to be associated with past frustration: "My bed of light is a furnace choking me/ With hell" (TCO, 25). Percussive undercutting is used throughout, and even *simple expunging* as in "Drink to me only with/ And the reader is carried away" (TCO, 25). The middle section of the poem is a meditation on man and his inability to grow in dignity. The image employed is that of a plant striving to be a tree. The Prufrockian lament follows: "But no doubt you have understood/ It all now and I am a fool" (TCO, 26). The poem culminates in apostrophes to the possible beloved: "Who are you, anyway?" (TCO, 27). Ashbery intimates bleak incomprehension of this scene of suffering:

> Because what does anything mean,
>
> The ivy and the sand? The boat
> Pulled up on the shore? Am I wonder,
> Strategically, and in the light
> Of the long sepulcher that hid death and hides me?
>   (TCO, 27)

The phrase "Am I wonder" is opaque or at least ambiguous, since it tends to break down syntactically into "Am I," "I wonder" or "Am, I wonder," etc. Various attempts to give this straightforward discursive *metaphrasis* are doomed, particularly since Ashbery in this "middle period" plays with the possibilities of these "mistakes" entering into the circumference of vision and meaning. The poem ends in an evocation of that ecstasy concerning the incomprehensibility of life and death, the "wonder, strategically" in which the poet finds himself again and again. Ashbery is a poet concerned with the ecstasy of not understanding, much in the way Kafka's "Philosopher Dog" is concerned with cognition: obsessively so, but structurally unable to pierce through to the "heart of the mystery." Just as a dog is tautologically unable to understand the "human" world, Ashbery's dwarf-man is structurally also unable to understand:

"in the light/ Of the long sepulcher that hid death and hides me?" (TCO, 27). It is not that mortality touches the mind but how it does not that makes the poet cry out. It is this light, the atmosphere of which "Some Trees" spoke ("Placed in a puzzling light, and moving" [ST, 51]), this puzzle, this labyrinth, into which Ashbery moves the reader. The poem rehearses its greatest pejoratives for those who think the familiar is too comprehensible, as in: "He is not a man/ Who can read these signs . . . his bones were stays . . ." (TCO, 26). The poem alternates its questions concerning mortality with certain pastoral-sexual reminiscences, paradigmatic of Ashbery's more eroticized moods:

> After which you led me to water
> And bade me drink, which I did, owing to your kindness.
> You would not let me out for two days and three nights,
> Bringing me books bound in wild thyme and scented wild grasses
> (TCO, 27)

Prufrockian self-laceration however is the upshot of this idyllic trial: "Now you are laughing./ Darkness interrupts my story./ Turn on the light" (TCO, 27). These self-lacerations seem to prove over and over again that happiness, sexually or cognitively, is structurally impossible for the *persona*. But the impossible poem, the only possibility, has already occurred.

"Rain" is yet another successful composition through abstract-impressionistic fragmentation. It is an evocation, like the long and later "Fragment" (DDS, 78) (comically, this "Fragment" is one of the longest of Ashbery's poems, just as the comically titled *Three Poems* are almost entirely written in prose, as if to show that even titles in Ashbery's worlds may also be presented merely to be lacerated; nothing in his poetic universe is free from parody), of an unhappy love affair. The affair is presented in that species of "shorthand" which seems at once like the

"Penelope" section of *Ulysses* in its associativeness and like the collage parts of *Paterson* in its "manufactured object" tone. "Rain" begins with an evocation in the comically humdrum fashion of Ashbery: "The spoon of your head" (TCO, 28). A menacing and haunting lyric follows: "You see only the white page its faint frame of red/ You hear the viola's death sound/ A woman sits in black and white tile// Why, you are pale" (TCO, 28). The funereal quality of these images is maintained throughout: "Cupped under the small lead surface of that cloud you see you are/ going to die/ . . . The day of the week will not save you" (TCO, 29).

The poem contains an almost Roman epigrammatic quality, as in the obituary-like irony of "And the little one/ the hooded lost one/ near the pillow/ A fine young man" (TCO, 31). This little demotic phrase becomes the prelude to an extraordinary climax of stormy impenetrability, a surrealist cadenza beginning with "The storm coming . . . the houses were vanishing behind a cloud . . . The flat sea rushing away" (TCO, 31). These images of collapse and speed are the terrifying molecules of a larger vision of funereal disproportion and unrelatedness. While some of the stanzas remind one of a truncated Reverdy ("calm/ Hat against the sky/ Eyes of forest" [TCO, 30]), and indeed seem to abound with moments that recall the early, simpler style, as in the "eyes of forest," the whole poem finally seems a fractured, dulled short story of disaster, in which, however, the sequentiality of the love affair has been dislocated.

This poem, however, must be distinguished from the lack of sequentiality in Ashbery's earlier dream poems. The poem "Rain" is not in Rimbaud's sense the work of the vatic poet, making himself ever more deranged in all senses. It is a domesticated, prosy version, and vision, with menacing overtones and a final disordered cadenza, of the memory of a brutal love affair. The best poets since Rimbaud behave like visionaries who have not yet seen the vision. This is their elegiac and anticipatory strength. Images seem explicitly to be derived from a daylight world of action ("The first coffee in the morning" [TCO, 29]), even though this time is much condensed, as in a dream: "Soon the stars" (TCO, 29). Here the narrative is obviously condensing to be more mimetic of the sudden ways of memory. Ashbery, like Proust, is concerned in most of his love poems, as in "The New Spirit," with meditation on the possible *survival* of the memories of love. In Ashbery's collages of love, not bits of *madeleines* ignite whole scenes, but a few words, a few newspaper images, ignite further incomprehensible wholes in a mauve vision. It is a vision like Proust's, culminating in grand collapses, but not until *Three Poems* is there any "ethical" indictment of the aesthetic way of perceiving and behaving itself. In the middle poems, Ashbery is largely concerned with an immediacy of presentation, even if what is presented is a rumination. Ashbery's immediacy, then, seems to be constantly bathed in a slight ambience of distantiation, a paradox which Ashbery achieves as by a certain varnish over bright paint, his prose interpolations almost "covering" the lyric, idyllic poetical moments.

Dream imagery in *The Tennis Court Oath* is radically reduced. The *collage* style permits an extraordinary amount of "waking" material: material, as in the prose poem "Idaho," seemingly dredged, lifted, and/or "cut-up" from cheap fiction, among other sources. Ashbery has admitted, in several interviews, the popular sources for "Europe" and other poems. "Idaho" seems almost utterly "lifted" *rather than parodied*, a "pop" object, as in: "During the past few months, Biff had become quite a frequent visitor to Carol's apartment./ He never failed to marvel at the cool, corrected elegance of the place as contrasted with its warm . . ." (TCO, 91). This prose style, the style reflecting a cheap fictional mode, not necessarily the only modality of everyday apprehension, but a dominant *if* demotic and coarsened one, can be compared to Ashbery's surreal prose in "The Ascetic Sensualists" (TCO, 51): "The least astonished were the wetter veterans who had come to pray and practice, unaware as yet that the basilica's southern tip was submerged—you to whom I write, can you believe them this instant far from ideal palms?" (TCO, 54). The diction of the last question is reminiscent of René Char's glamorous tone in his war journals, austere yet always sensuous. This is "poetic" prose, and Ashbery in his collages constantly compares this literary tone with the flatter quality of popular fiction: "The aviator and his/ observer climbed out of the seats and stood/ with Mr. Aylesworth, chatting and laughing" (TCO, 73), and the flatter quality of certain scientistic, urbanistic, or technological descriptions: "As pipes decorate laminations of/ City unit busses pass through" (TCO, 90). In "Idaho" the flat narrative is fractured only by cheap "endless" question marks ("???????????????????????????" [TCO, 91]) and abrupt mid-progress shifts pointing up always the cheap mystery-story motif of sudden death. The style mimics the action, explosively; just as the cheap fiction explodes from its sluggishness into all-too-expected collapse, the modern artist follows the original narrative and then fractures it with unexpected, yet by now characteristic, lacerations.

The Tennis Court Oath is a book of extreme dissociation, and the 111-part poem "Europe" is the masterpiece of a ruptured collagiste style. "Europe," like W. C. Williams' *Paterson*, is constructed in a style which expresses all textures, dictions, and voices: but, unlike *Paterson*, it proceeds with a quickening tempo, and its description is not the affirmation of a rootedness within a city which is a world, as in *Paterson*, but the desiccation within an entire continent which is but a microcosm. W. C. Williams offers love lyrics, histories of industry, journalistic snatches, letters (the famous Allen Ginsberg epistle from the '40s), all to show that the seemingly "low" subject of Paterson has within it the seeds of salvation and *communitas*. Williams indicates that even the lowliest of New Jersey scapes can be redeemed by the fine eye of the physician-poet, and that this is as fine a subject as the elite tradition of his colleague and former mentor Pound. Ashbery has selected, as his title indicates, postwar Europe and/or a subway stop in contemporary Paris as the scale on which to indicate the unredeemedness, the humorous horror, disruption of tradition, and disruption of traditional norms in relationships with nature and machine. The menacing domination of mechanical dictions and machines themselves is not seen patiently or lovingly but in a disjunct manner which indicates the abstract expressionist urge toward smudged simultaneities of presentation. Williams' humor is gentle and loving, as in the lascivious dialogues of the last parts of *Paterson* (p. 189), the bucolic parodied; but Ashbery's parodies are presented as parts of a "new reality," the heartlessly banal, not yet seen as "precious" or redemptive, but presented in its brutal dullness. Only Williams' "Pure products of America" approaches the *terribilità* of "Europe" and it lacks Ashbery's motley range and dismal hues.

Like the "meaningless" mumblings that terminate "The Hollow Man," actually the *persona* groping to remember the Lord's Prayer, "Europe" begins with several poems that seem to try to indicate a possible *lyric of chaos*, but the surrealism has become extraordinarily muted, the ecstatic dream moment is lacerated in the businesslike tones of "To employ her/ construction ball" (TCO, 64). Little moments of André Breton-like surrealist ecstasy are juxtaposed with moments of nauseated incoherence:

> Morning fed on the
> light blue wood
> of the mouth
>   cannot understand
> feels deeply)
>   (TCO, 64)

Minimalism, a movement in art which tended toward the blank and geometrical, is prophesied in Ashbery's rigorous economies of presentation: "a wave of nausea—/ numerals" (TCO, 64). Pop Art was often predicated on the *simple* image, as in Jasper Johns' targets, alphabets, numerals, and flags; images that were ambiguous precisely because the presentation was so literal: the subject always flat and geometrical and given. Ashbery's poem seems to present literal slices of life, but a life pulverized into a few isolated words, not even freshened up like the *Tender Buttons* of Gertrude Stein, and not rhythmically reiterated: "a few berries" (TCO, 64). The words often manneristically discuss the jerkiness of the poet's transitions in a world of speedy dissections: "The background of poles roped over/ into star jolted them" (TCO, 64). The poet has dropped connectives, *copulas*, and syntax itself in an effort, not as in E. E. Cummings to produce an ecstatic *allegro*, but to emphasize the *dérèglement de tous les sens* of a colossal *Ennui*. The ecstatic is presented only to be brutally erased. One thinks of the "leaving-out business" of "The Skaters" in these lines from "Europe": "What might have/ children singing/ the horses" (TCO, 64), which seems to be the shards of a *possible* phrase, such as: "What might have been the scene of children singing on the circus horses."

The problem of a poem of disrupted syntax is indicated by the failure of Pound in the *Cantos* to present a principle of cohesion. Ashbery was forced to consider how to unify a composition whose subject was disunity. If unifying intentions become too apparent, the theme of discontinuity is merely artificially presented with a pleasing frame. Ashbery employs a parsimonious distribution of a few narrative elements throughout the poem, as well as an interpolation of sudden songlike elements, with a closure indicating both narrative recapitulation and final discontinuity. The poem is not vitiated as a poem of *ennui*, "sinful" despair, lapsed *eros*, insidious technology, contingency and camp; but the contingency is presented within a poem of a certain "construction." Monotony itself is somewhat betrayed by its most concrete representation. The poem is a repetitive prayer of reification.

Throughout the poem prose sections are presented from a now impossible-to-locate, cheap book which Ashbery affirms he discovered on the quais of Paris: *Beryl of the Bi-Planes*. Its placid plane imagery moved him, just as he is moved by the despairingly inarticulate two-dimensionalisms of comic books and cheap prints (tastes he shares with the classic Rimbaldien catalogue of cheap tastes in *Saison en Enfer*). "Alongside" this narrative is another concerning a Ronald Pryor and Collins, who are seen in speeding cars on a Great North Road. Suspense and coherence are mocked in the transitions presented without sequitur: "All was now ready for the continuance of the journey." Like the newspaper passages of *Ulysses*, the sudden mid-progress shifts remind us of the Aeolian nonsensicality of the "old-fashioned cause-and-effect" of cheap novels.

"Europe" contains Ashbery's usual self-tangled passages, in the third and first person, though the first person is never easily synonymous with the poet, since the shifty shifters merely float upon the page in the extreme discomfort of a shattered diary: "I moved up/ glove/ the field" (TCO, 67). "He had mistaken his book for garbage" is a complete part (part 10, p. 65), and it is the antilyrical antithesis of the single-lined melodies of early works. Melody is eschewed for the "prepared piano" effects of John Cage, who was at this time an inspiration for Ashbery in his grand example of employing noise and colloquial "unmusical" effects within a field of indeterminacy. "The Waste Land" is conjured in an oxymoron of hideous construction: "Before the waste/ went up" (TCO, 66). The waste is seen as *piling up*, just as absences in "The Skaters" are said to leave bitter impressions, are indeed substantial absences, so in "Europe," the waste itself remains and destroys. Remorse itself is presented as dried up, as in the seduction scene of "The Waste Land" and Baudelaire's "Au Lecteur": "she left the room, oval tear tonelessly fell" (TCO, 67). One may contrast these toneless tears with the lyrical, surrealist ecstasy of "The Poems" in which the dawn is likened to a tear that drops from a smiling person. Here the pathetic fallacy is abandoned, and excruciating montage acts *against* the persona, shutting him out: "She was dying but had time for him—/ brick" (TCO, 68). The theme of helpless incoherence is presented in part 30: "More upset, wholly meaningless, the willing sheath/ glide into fall . . mercury to passing/ the war you said won" (TCO, 69). The *terribilità* in the elided syntax of *the war winning* is contrasted unexpectedly with the next classical intrusion: "And somehow the perfect warrior is fallen" (TCO, 69). As in Jasper Johns, Tennyson is merely a word.

The plane imagery and the parachutes remind the reader not only of the intrusion of sleek machines, but of pre-World War I imagery. The poet feels nostalgic about this epoch and contrasts it gloomily with contemporary horror. The "Pop" artists often received with celebratory irony the Hollywood movies of the thirties because of the beguiling image of escapist spectacle and untrammeled hedonism, and Ashbery delights in the unworried prose and atmosphere of the girls of the bi-plane.* "It was in German. The aviator and his/ observer climbed out of the seats and stood/ with Mr. Aylesworth, chatting and laughing" (TCO, 73). Somehow, however, the perfect warrior is not only fallen but incoherent; the shards do not constitute the cubist presentation of a unified city, as in *Paterson* or *The Bridge*, but the "New Realist" presentation of an almost utterly erased *communitas*, and without the saving dignity and pietistic canons of

---

* Koch's "airplane" novel, *The Red Robins*, proved that there is a real Santa Claus, the unreal one of poetry and language.

"The Waste Land." There are, in "Europe," almost *no traces of a literary past* except the literature of the masses or of children, rejected literatures that the poet rehabilitates for ironic purposes. "The Lord's Prayer" cannot even intrude onto this desolate scene: "The rose/ dirt/ dirt you/ pay" (TCO, 73). Slogans and clichés, moreover, are presented "whole," for while all else is scattered, pulverized, and shattered, the clichés can be presented in their agonizing integrity: "He is probably one of the gang" (TCO, 74). All else ends as quickly as a sleeping Pompeii: "Mood seems the sort/ to brag/ end." Closure itself has lost dignity. The epic is presented not with the erotic curves which Poe thought the only proper intervals of a long poem. Closure comes almost randomly, to indicate that one proceeds, with as much risk as the Sartrean being perched above the abyss, from particular to particular, never capable of the general, without verifications or principles, without the Eliotic, the Arnoldian touchstones, and swamped by the sordid without insight: "beginning to get tired you realize," part 58 *ends* (TCO, 75).

"Beginning to get tired you realize": a paradigmatic phrase that *lacks an object*. The poet too presents a world without normative rapports: "He came over the hill/ He held me in his arms—it was marvelous.// But the map of Europe/ shrinks around naked couples" (TCO, 74). The sudden lyric is inverted: "Precise mechanisms/ Love us" (TCO, 74), and bestiality is replaced by the curious inversion of machines loving loveless men. This songlike intrusion is ironically the height of relation and Buberian "Thou" in "Europe," in which solipsism, "each in his prison," is the reigning configuration. Sudden death pursues erotics in an Elizabethan pun: "Even as you lick the stamp/ A brown dog lies down beside you and dies" (TCO, 74). The height of love is reached and contrasted with "blinding banality": "We are not more loved than now/ The newspaper is ruining your eyes" (TCO, 74). Not so much sudden blindness as the irritation and chafing of despair against a world of "mimetic" newspapers: "Lenin de Gaulle three days later/ also comparing simple" (TCO, 75), in which the simplicities of journalism, and the simplicities of inane everyday, public coherence, are suddenly jumbled and seen as menacing and maniacal.

Into the darkness of this poem comes not the eclectic illuminators, the Sanskrit anecdotalists, that illuminate "The Waste Land" and "Four Quartets," but the "New Realism" of "searchlights" and their uncoded messages. The poem begins with misunderstood messages, and throughout entertains the theme of slashed dialogue and ruptured narrative, but throughout also there are distributed tiny images of mechanical light, that somehow "pierce the darkness, skyward" (TCO, 84) if only to flicker seemingly meaningless "puzzle pictures": the miniature searchlight of part 111; the searchlight sweeping in 93; the glow of the little electric light bulb in 37. These are configurations of "realistic," mechanical light. Light in John Ashbery's middle period is almost never the metaphysical light of Eliot, nor is his darkness a metaphysical symbol of decay. The light that pierces the sky of Europe may be taken allegorically, but the poem is certainly going a long way toward making any congruence between characters or images and symbolic substances difficult and uncertain.

The *personae* are "merely" lifted from the "everymen" of cheap commercial novels. This may not stop the reader however from responding to the characters as affectionate two-dimensional *reminders* of the more traditional "Everyman." The "message" at the closure of "Europe" is not a fragment of well-known literary texts, as in the closure of Eliot, but it seems *to allude* to this possibility in its Morse flashes and flares, "N.F., N.F." (TCO, 85). This closure, like the stars presented at the close of "The Skaters," seems to have perfect dramatic sense, but its sense is its very nonsensicality, lack of depth or refer-

ence. The message is presented so smoothly in the recapitulation of the Ronald Pryor story that one is led liquidly into
thinking that a decoding process, the detection of coherence, is
about to be deployed. But the poem ends in a sentence fragment, a mere noun, though one seeming to indicate, through
curious metonymy, the endurance of life within this bright
black void: "the breath" (TCO, 85).

The light that terminates the poem "Europe" is peculiarly
"winking" and in succession it flashes sadly the impure acrostics
of an undecoded riddle: "N.F., N.F." (TCO, 85). Poetry in our
age is detective story or science fiction without keys. As opposed to purity there is "Another five minutes passed in darkness" (TCO, 85), and though the scale is as grand as the format
of a Willem deKooning, the presentation is of a dry and un-
yielding waste: "Dry, the bush/ settling Everybody" (TCO, 84).
The *calligrammes* of Apollinaire used concrete mimesis manneristically to "duplicate" images of rain. Ashbery's part 104
employs a grid system only to indicate disruption and "meaningless" framing:

104.

blaze			aviators	
	out		dastardly	

However, this suddenly minimal *calligramme* suggests the tense
personalist isolations within this void.

Dream imagery in Ashbery's early poems was often a result of
Keatsian and surrealist escapism into a world of wishes. Ecstatic
fulfillments and bizarre disappointments could be dramatically
deployed in poems of a Wallace Stevensesque hedonistic "glam-
our." In "Europe" the dream has been shattered, like the
mountains of Cézanne. The poet has presented incongruous

dreams, *grotesqueries* of desire and dread, but there the grotesque is of the literal world, the concrete and matter-of-fact: Lenin, de Gaulle. The friendly giants of the early works have become an intrusion of "fancy": "This was the third thing/ another giant" (TCO, 82). Nausea is presented not because of the voluptuous frustrations within nightmare, but because of the *tedium vitae* of the businesslike world. The aesthetic methodology is not the enthralled world of *Les Illuminations* but the drabber rejections of a Henry Green novel. The memories of dreams are now "literary objects" such as collaged cheap novels, with their cheapened suspense and coherence. The poet does not merely dream that his work is rejected, as in the nightmare of "The Poems"; now his distrust is presented in daylight idiom: "He had mistaken his book for garbage" (TCO, 65). Deaths are not the rituals of an elegant suicide, as in *Some Trees* (p. 48), but the horrifying ceremonies of the fully wakened souls: "gosh flowers upset ritual" (TCO, 65). Wanderings and tergiversations are possible within a world of picaresque and purple prose, but the poet has rejected bathetic quests: "You cannot illusion; the dust" (TCO, 67). The generalized fancies of metaphysics are not even paraded but mightily assembled and mocked: "abstract vermin the garden worn smiles" (TCO, 67). So much for any allusion to the garden in Eliot; and flying too is not presented as an erotic occasion or the Yeatsian political one of courage and catastrophe. It is barely business, just another phenomenon, framed by cheap prose, in a colorless indifferent universe.

Why should one bother with such seemingly meaningless collages? In "Europe," we find a work that seems to come less to "the sense of an ending" than to the ending of sense, and yet it has an overwhelming value as "intellectual music." Its broken sentences break the rules to create the most dramatic of exceptions, and its cohesive passages, lifted from a cheap novel, have a poignant transparency and inexhaustible wit as parodistic specimens. The poem's discontinuous stream of consciousness points to what clinicians might call a state of "schizoid disruption," but here all is organized and sinuously linked by Ashbery's beautiful threadlike connections. The disjunctions speak to us of a state of ontological insecurity, and this brave use of disjunction seems the most effective vehicle for a poem concerned with large private and public trauma. Like "The Waste Land," its *disjecta membra* is part of a poetically pragmatic presentation of a deformed and abnormal condition. Ashbery, like Eliot, knows how to employ dissonance sensuously, and all his fragmented bits combine finally in a savage burlesque, a kind of rhapsody to failure, economical for all its incoherence. Disjunction, parody, collage, may not necessarily be regressions and anomalies, but a normative response to an uncertain universe, a negative response to a culture of commodities.

Thus, Ashbery concludes with a grand masterpiece his bleak period of collage. The lessons of collage, like the devices of the surrealists used in the early works, are never completely lost in the later works. The alert reader of *Rivers and Mountains, The Double Dream of Spring*, and later work will constantly notice those elements of collage in seemingly witty, neoclassical pieces. A flat newspaper tone often betrays the attitude of the *collagiste*, if not the methodology of one. Collage has always been associated, in the other arts, with *trompe-l'oeil*, and thus parody, and it is to parody most that Ashbery turns in his later works, if only to annihilate by its total use the very idea of parody. His all-inclusive parodistic tone is different from the bleak, "cheap" collages of *The Tennis Court Oath* in that often a "higher" tone is synthetically managed. But those tones, those voices, too, are distinctively borrowed, as in collage. The theme of discontinuity and collapse, so underlined in *The Tennis Court Oath*, is developed, but with a newer emphasis on forms of belief along with disbelief. The dramatic immediacy of the collages of *The Tennis Court Oath* is, however, never equalled, and it seems that its particular disjunct style had, for the author, reached its limit. From here on, he concerns himself with searching for different principles of cohesion. But to reject these experimental and vital works for the later syntheses is slightly like abusing "les Demoiselles d'Avignon" from the point of view of Picasso's later neoclassicism. Squeamish sensibilities flee this cubo-futurism too fast.

CHAPTER 4

The Poetry of Parody: Rivers and Mountains

The volume *Rivers and Mountains,* published in 1966, contains twelve poems concluding with the gigantic "The Skaters." The volume in this sense is Eliotic, relying on the "masterwork" to offset the actual paucity of lyrics included, and in this sense the volume looks forward to *Three Poems,* in which the poet entirely eschews the presentation of smaller, less ambitious work, for even the "small" scale of "The Recital" is vast (12 pages) when one is reminded of the usual line length of Ashbery's lyric poems. Ashbery's development is thus not toward drama, as is often the case with poets, but toward the extended soliloquy, the meditational confession, or "visionary" modality, as with Stevens and Eliot.

"These Lacustrine Cities" (RAM, 9) is a powerful poem using the theme of urban horror to expose a form of writing and being. The rare phrase, "lacustrine cities" is balanced by the quotidian force of the "redundancy": "that man is horrible, *for instance,/* Though this is only *one example"* (RAM, 9; italics mine). Here the feminine endings produce a certain suspenseful cadence. The cities *re-present* the central theme of the second

stanza, which has the fine paradox: "all that hate was transformed into useless love" (RAM, 9). The central and abiding
theme here seems to be one of the "ascending emptiness" of the
urban artificiality of language itself, and the concomitant interior sense of emptiness on the part of the persona. A self-
lacerating and parodistic "we" announces insidiously, perhaps to
the reader, perhaps to the poet, in Chinese-box manner, "we
have all-inclusive plans for you" (RAM, 9). A solipsistic "solution" is posed by the poet towards the conclusion of the poem:
"the past is already here, and you are nursing some private project" (RAM, 9). Once again, Ashbery represents the frustration
of the poet within his enchanting escapism: "pressing you back
into a startled dream/ As sea-breezes greet a child's face" (RAM,
9). This line represents a feminine ending or spondee, depend-
ing upon *voicing,* and the long e's build to an extraordinary
Keatsian melody of assonance: "Dream/ As *sea*-breezes greet a
child's face." The theme of *terror* is given in the insidious line
"The worst is not over, yet I know/ You will be happy here"
(RAM, 9). A kind of Orwellian *Newspeak* ("War is peace") reminds us of the later *acedia* and *dumps* of the poet in "The
Skaters." The poem is a Proustian prophecy of the cracks in the
ivory tower and the possibility that the labyrinthine project (the
"mountain of something . . . this single monument" [RAM, 9])
is not in the least a "pleasure dome" of Kubla Khan proportions,
but indeed an Ozymandian modality: "Whose wind is desire
starching a petal,/ Whose disappointment broke into a rainbow
of tears" (RAM, 9). The poet has taken urban discontinuity, and
urban monumentality, and gracefully, within a small-scaled,
though rather toughly arched and controlled quatrain modality,
has created a *Klage* or Rilkesque lament on the "City of Pain."
The poet tends to be seen as analogous here to the anonymous
and malevolent genius "behind" and "in" the city. The "idea"
that "man is horrible" is indeed the Christian sense of *original*

sin that haunts the remorseful poetics of discontinuity in this new period of Ashbery. The poet's condemnation of the idea seems weak. *Agape* is not the principle sought here; the word *love* itself is condemned for its weakness: "useless." Ashbery here playfully deposes the poetics of labyrinths himself: "Much of your time has been occupied by creative games" (RAM, 9). But the sense of a long, Kafkaesque journey without terminus is invoked.

It is interesting to note that in his more mature style, Ashbery tends to rescue any bleak closure with almost classic cadence. "Whose wind is desire starching a petal,/ Whose disappointment broke into a rainbow of tears" (RAM, 9). Here, the disappointment is paradoxically made lyrically fragrant and aesthetically iridescent, so that even in this poem of urban horror a species of radiant energy issues from the poet's frustration. This radiant, new lyricism is characteristic of the poems in *Rivers and Mountains*, not simply the glamorous dislocations of the early works, and neither the utterly bleak fragments of *The Tennis Court Oath*, but a synthesis, a new flourish.

The title poem, "Rivers and Mountains" (RAM, 10–12), is a "detective" poem, reminiscent of Roussel's drab poems of endless maniacal length. It is a poem without parenthetical mania, to be sure, but whose mania is the opacity with which a seemingly "simple narrative" is offered, deflected, deformed. The poem begins with an insidious scene of conspiracy: "On the secret map the assassins/ Cloistered, the Moon River was marked" (RAM, 10)—but a hyphenated *non sequitur* quickly leads the reader "away": "wan ending/ Of the trial among dry, papery leaves" (RAM, 10). Edgar Allan Poe's raven seems to be alluded to in mock-gothic: "The bird flew over and/ Sat—there was nothing else to do" (RAM, 10). The paradox of the map is now introduced, the figure being that of Borges' legendarily precise cartographers, who extended their maps in scale until the map reached the proportions of the country: "you found/ It all on paper but the land/ Was made of paper" (RAM, 10). All of writing's Gaul is divided into secrets. But the riddle is not so much disclosed as thickened by catalogues of public imagery: "major tax assessment area" (RAM, 11). The third stanza introduces the military schema, the possible disjunction of an army, which "worked well on paper/ But their camp had grown/ To be the mountains and the map/ Carefully peeled away" (RAM, 11). Ashbery's poem ends with the grand artifice of a monstrous dream landscape: "the affliction of June ride/ Slowly out into the sun-blackened landscape" (RAM, 12), but the reader is left with a dishevelled narrative, and an "unassassinated president's desk" (RAM, 12). Unassassinated, because clearly the "attempt" does not work: aesthetic humiliation and defeat accompanies the poem with its "wan ending" ironically transformed to a "sun-blackened" scape. The age of the funerals of Kennedy and King has not plucked the heart of its own mystery yet.

The reader is placed in the position of deciding whether this is "patent" nonsense, but one decides that Ashbery has given us a "map," a "score" in which the sensuous illusion of the minute particulars, "Scooping snow off the mountains rinsing" (RAM, 11), is enough to save the poem from mere shattered narrative. Detection appeals to Ashbery, as to Borges and Kafka, for many reasons, among them the fact that suspense, when causality itself is called in question, becomes the most obviously degraded or purely formal archaistic resource. Suspense, the idea of "what's next?" becomes a sensuous target for the poet. Not that the poet eschews all coherence, but he implies, by his perturbed narration in "Rivers and Mountains," a drama of "non-assassination," that the contemporary lament can be most uniquely evocative when it is framed in the most seemingly ontologically "secure" manner. What occurs may be a mere *manner*, but Ashbery seems to be a disciple of Borges' prose and utilizes Borges' dissolution of *genres* and parody of *the detective mode* to raise and then crush the "suspenseful" tonalities of his poetry.

On the whole, however, "Rivers and Mountains" seems a disappointment. Its various images do not interestingly coalesce or dramatically fall apart. While one can understand its parody of the detective mode, it seems a weakened compromise between the middle collage pieces and the neoclassic wit of "The Skaters." It lacks the strong stanzaic pull of "These Lacustrine Cities" and its drift toward a conclusion in landscape does not seem completely convincing or satisfactory.

"Last Month" is a beautiful lyric in which the enclosed garden of the Northern Renaissance painters seems to be visualized: "And in the garden, cries and colors" (RAM, 13). A form of annunciation in Northern Renaissance art is often accompanied by the juxtaposition of the most homely elements (the Madonna as peasant) and the regal aspects of the divine immanence. In the Ashbery poem, the beginning is grey and homely: "No changes of support—only/ Patches of gray, here where sunlight fell" (RAM, 13). But the eschatological hopes are enunciated in true surrealist fashion in the sudden: "The academy of the future is/ Opening its doors and willing" (RAM, 13). The image of light in Northern Renaissance iconography often signified the capacity of the divine to break through without rupture, as in the prototype of the Virgin Birth. Ashbery's new, natural light is "fruitless sunlight" streaming through (perhaps geodesic) "domes," and "timeless value" is compared with the more worthless novelty of "a new automobile/ ping pong set and garage" (RAM, 13). But the poem has a sacred dialectic, and ends with "the thief/ Stole everything like a miracle" (RAM, 13). The most discursive *metaphrasis* is that the poet is sensuously apprehending the beauty of loss of possessions, of sacrifice, the Epictetus-like cry that one can lose everything but one's immortal soul: the ping pong set is stolen, but in the garden, cries and colors remain the "timeless value" (RAM, 13). "Last Month" is ironically a chiliastic poem in the classic surrealist vein, and it is also a poem ironically entitled in honor of the past, which is seen substantially as a poem about the future. This is what Walter Benjamin called for: "profane illumination."

The cult of the future in Ashbery is one of the chief new elements of tension in the otherwise "wan ending of defeat and humiliation" that elsewhere presides. Property as value is not so much condemned as visually deployed in impressionistic "splotches" so that the sudden values of light ("A match recedes, slowly, into the night" [RAM, 13]), with a Reverdyesque isolation, may be thus more heightened. Ashbery in his youth was a painter, and has narrated that he became proficient in one kind of golden halo employed in sacred pictures by the Dutch.[1] In Ashbery's *Rivers and Mountains* period, for the first time, the contagion of sacred and profane qualities is kept at a maximum, and the poet is seemingly always close to meditational confession (as in "Clepsydra," [RAM, 28–30]) in a rather specifically *theological* vein, and there is the possibility of a "Hollow Man" attitude as in the despair of "The Skaters": "Sleep, death and hollyhocks" (RAM, 53). "Last Month," too, could well be thought of iconographically as a small-scaled allusion to a saintly fight against temptations to despair (or to believe). Ashbery often seems to be insisting on a need for "instruction." The subject of a need for authority is alluded to in the eschatology of "The academy of the future" (RAM, 13). The poet seems to be wandering in his *Rivers and Mountains* work away from an intransigeant attitude against the academic and settled, and is appealing, as was Eliot in his middle work, for a possible reclamation of archaistic "timeless value." Like the early Eliot of "The Hippopotamus," however, he is certainly the first to be able to parody the connotatively encrusted accounts of these "values."

Ashbery's "Civilization and Its Discontents" (RAM, 14) is a poem of lucid despair, ending with the present participles of hope, "Cutting swamps for men like lapdogs, holding its own,/ Performing once again, for you and for me" (RAM, 15). Sigmund Freud's *Civilization and Its Discontents*[2] is a work of extreme intransigeance; it is late Freud's most dark dicta on the problem of the claims, in conflict, of his structures of ego and id, culture and instinctual force. In the Ashbery poem, the Freudian tag serves to remind us of his "pessimistic" vein. The sentence fragments begin with a large-scale, Freudian image of men chained to impulse: "A people chained to aurora/ I alone disarming you" (RAM, 14). The "disarmament" image reminds one of Ashbery's characteristic wit, in which an embrace might be seen as a disarmament, and also suggests Freud's rejection of any mere pacifism, due to his dark knowledge of impulse. Ashbery once again uses the word "miracle." Here it is the erotic *miracle*, or Buberian grace, of *relation*. Immediately, it is juxtaposed with images of nostalgia: "In that other time, when you and I were young" (RAM, 14). Clichés are mounted as if in Freudian defense. Civilization and waking life are sustained only as a form of strychnine: "I had already swallowed the poison/ And could only gaze into the distance at my life/ Like a saint's with each day distinct" (RAM, 15).

The poem ends, like Goethe's *Faust* Part II, with images of reclamation, and the almost positive ending will be a feature of almost all of Ashbery's more mature works on the *ethos* and *mythos* of discontinuity. "The Skaters" ends with the stars; the poem-collage "Europe," with "the breath"; "The New Spirit" employs cosmic order again in the Kantian sense (the moral order within; the starry heavens above); "The System's" end is the hope for "a pragmatic and kinetic" future; and "The Recital" concludes with language of something "intimate and noble" left after *desire for this dignity* is removed. These mature conclu-

sions point to the ironic figure of the "starry heavens" ("gaze
into the distance" [RAM, 15]) because for Ashbery the heavens
are not a medieval map signifying an allegorical interpretation of
moral order. Ashbery refers to a colorless indifferent universe,
and his endings, no matter how positive, must be seen often as
sonata-like returns to a C major that ever more forcefully sets
off in dark relief the mysterious disjunctions and atonalities of
the works themselves. The curious order of the "distance" and
"stars" may be seen as only a homogeneous streaming, similar
to that deposed by critics considering the random effects of abstract expressionism. Likewise, the reclamation imagery, the
Freudian compromise at the end of "Civilization and Its Discontents" may be a kind of Keatsian awakening from sleep but is
replete and enthralled as if with disaster: "wan ending" "of humiliation and defeat" (RAM, 10). It is bleakly possible that the
starry conclusions, along with the pragmatic or chiliastic hopes
for the future, are mere parodies, as in the obviously parodistic
line: "The night, and the stars, and the way we used to be"
(RAM, 14). Ashbery's conclusions are drastic *attempts at closure*
in an open-ended universe.

"Civilization and Its Discontents" does finally affirm, in Pasternak's simple sense, domestic life itself, and in a canonically
rural setting. "Only life under the huge trees/ Like a coat that
has grown too big, moving far away." Life, animated and redemptive, is finally the comic hero ("Cutting swamps for men
like lapdogs" [RAM, 15]) of the poem, just as Eros is the hero of
all of Freud's work. The poem is confusing because so much
nostalgia, hermeticism, solipsism, and public imagery is confused together, and not in some simple, drab way. But the recurrent verbs of the ending remind one of the affirmative nature
of the theme, however darkened by impulse and conflict: "moving . . . cutting swamps . . . holding its own . . . performing
once again" (RAM, 15). And here, the "you" of the poem seems

inspiringly three-dimensional and the persona reasserts, if only in parodied nostalgia, his own three-dimensionality. Thus, in the mature works, with "life" at the center, in all its probabilistics and conflict, Ashbery can reassert himself as a possible love poet. Recall, too, it is the life of rewriting Ashbery reaffirms.

An emblem of the multifoliate charm, the randomlike streaming, and the vital desire for order, is given in Ashbery's formulaic poem, "Into the Dusk-Charged Air" (RAM, 17). This poem is built on "rules" of rivers, the poem becoming a map and *catalogue raisonné* in much the way Joyce employed his rivers in *Finnegans Wake*, except that here the weaving is more bare, and *only* the rivers and weather remain. What is important to note is that the poem is not simply a Whitmanesque catalogue for the sake of *scale*, nor is it merely a Rousselian *tour de force* of interesting drabness, nor is it merely wilful. The poem is reminiscent, in a bizarre fashion, of Pasternak's reliance in *Dr. Zhivago* on imagery of weather. Ashbery's haunting rivers are glimpsed as impersonally as a Lucretian vision might allow, and we are in the grips of a "chilling" naturalism, terminally chilling, in fact, as the poem ends with a catalogue of ice: "The Oka is frozen solider/ . . . The Minho slumbers/ In winter . . . The Dvina soaks up the snow/ . . . the Adige's frozen . . ." (RAM, 20). It concludes: "The Ardèche glistens feebly through the freezing rain." Ashbery's poem, which begins with the overflowing Irawaddy, is a paradigm of a contemporary discussion of physical entropy. The image of harmony ("the Rhine sings its eternal song" [RAM, 17]) is presented in harmonic metrics of *decasyllabics*, with a nonclassical second foot caesura, to be sure. But the poem ends with a deliberate and spellbinding accretion of concrete particulars of "defeat" in wintry death that rivals Stevens' "Snow Man." The poem is orchestral and grand, and is not, in Eliot's phrase, "violated by an idea." Poetry here is impure flow.

One of the few love poems, seamlessly so, in Ashbery's canon is the poem entitled "A Blessing in Disguise" (RAM, 26). (One of the few, except that all his poetry is a Proustian lament.) Ashbery here uses a cliché for title that unexpectedly is freshened in the light of the poem's theme of disjunction, disassociation, and affirmation among concealments and camouflage. The poem was meant to end parodistically in the tones of an intelligent *homme moyen sensuel,* but actually the poem does not revel that heavily in any of the parodistic snobbisms that that tone would indicate.

The piece begins with a sudden eleven-syllable line, with a truncated iamb followed by two dactyls ("théy aře ălíve aňd căn háve") and two iambs or one spondee and iamb: this gives a sense of the rich variety of rhythmical interpretations that can be accorded to the rich first line: "Yes, they are alive and can have those colors." This is followed by the jubilant: "But I, in my soul, am alive too" (RAM, 26). The problem here is that the poet is employing a vocabulary precariously close to the utterly sentimental and passé, the question for the follower of Ashbery's poetics being: when will the *blunder* into sentiment be shown to be the first "chess" move in an *obvious* parody. The chance for this revision, to see the poet lacerate old vocabulary in an obviously playful way, comes with lines six and seven: "to sing of me/ Which are you" (RAM, 26). The poet begins to fall into charming clumsinesses, like comedic purposeful slips: "I should never have expected, *or suspected,* perhaps" (RAM, 26; italics mine). The poem's imagery of erotic dissolution, couched in the vocabulary of the clichés of love lyrics, reminds us that the theme of "dérèglement de tous les sens," and "je est un autre" has not been abdicated by the poet as his usual opening and conclusion. Rimbaud's dissociation is explicitly alluded to in the last quatrain: "I prefer 'you' in the plural, I want 'you' " (RAM, 26), but the poem ends with a line of combined colloquial and literary porphyry: "And then I start getting this feeling of exaltation" (RAM, 26). Ashbery employs landscape here in order to get the advantage out of the "pathetic fallacy" while parodying it: "The great spruces loom . . . the chairs ever/ Have their backs turned to the light/ Inflicted on the stone and paths, the real trees// That seem to shine at me through a lattice toward you" (RAM, 26). The whole exercise of style is filled with a Hamletic use of "seems": "expected, or suspected, perhaps," "That *seem* to shine," "*If* the wild light of this January day is true" (RAM, 26; italics mine). The subjunctive is used as a form of witty nonagreement: "If the wild light of this January day is true/ I pledge me to be truthful unto you" (RAM, 26). This whole exercise in the loving "lie" reminds one of the classical *topos* in the Sonnets of Shakespeare, concerned with the puns on lying, sex, and flattery.

The poem is an obvious flattery: "You must come to me, all golden and pale/ Like the dew and the air" (RAM, 26). The archaic furniture or imagery, the chairs in the light, the spruce, the wild January light, and the dew and the air, are juxtaposed to make a nonsense landscape in which only the loving innovation remains. One takes the line, "I prefer 'you' in the plural" (RAM, 26) as a reference to the nonintimate Gallic form, in which case the lover eschews the more usual *tutoyer* of the love lyric for the almost fetishistic distantiation. Distance and *lack of gratification* is a theme of Ashbery's poems we have examined in a number of cases: the dwarf of "How Much Longer" (TCO, 25), the distance between Dido and Aeneas in the self-consuming "Two Sonnets" (TCO, 20). The poet is full of synacsthetic landscape ("wild light" and "pastel girth of the day") and distorted hedonism ("I prefer 'you' in the plural, I want 'you' "). The wit of the "plural" is saturnalian, and celebratory. In any case, the quatrains are an achievement in a contemporary *eros* of disjunction, paradoxical scenes, and canonical irresolutions.

The parodistic element in "A Blessing in Disguise" (RAM, 26) should not be necessarily seen as merely self-lacerating. For Ashbery, the poem remains, it is true, as very much a parody of sentiment, but this wistful mannered replica of feeling is something which the poet finally affirms. While it is important to see that the poet is not utterly committed to a psychological narration, a three-dimensional Thou, it is equally important to sense the only slightly veiled desire to somehow get "out" of the literary framework and address a "you" more or less "naturally." But this is impossible, and Ashbery knows it more richly than anyone. Within Ashbery's extreme self-consciousness, however, any species of naturalism is necessarily condemned to be parodied, at the best. But the playful desire for the archaic form of a "love sonnet" reproduces, no matter how percussively decorated with clumsy effects, something of the feeling-tone of a positive mode. This is the newly balanced tone of the *Rivers and Mountains* period.

CHAPTER 5

"The Skaters": An Analysis

"The Skaters" does not proceed, like the collage poem "Europe," from opacity to opacity, but rather from parody to parody. Based on the comically cheap book, *Three Hundred Things a Bright Boy Can Do,*[1] it is a modulated collage on the ambiguous amusements of solitary mind. It is a poem of deracination, of the "professional exile," not however the totally crushed exile of "Europe," but a figure haunting a fine labyrinth for the possibility of *logos.* At the end, one is offered a scene of the starry heavens, but now overtly haphazard and strangely probabilistic. Contingency is, however, finally affirmed. It is a subtle affirmation.

While the poem contains a multitude of parodistic targets and sources, each of its four major parts contains a dominant parody or parodied feeling-tone. The opening stanza seems largely a parody of Eliot. The "violet air" and "stumps of time" from "The Waste Land" seem suggested in the "violet seeming" and "stumps" of this passage, and the frantic philosophical analysis that ends with "perdition" more than echoes Eliot's tone from "The Waste Land" to "Four Quartets." Part II is dominated by an exotic voyage in Baudelaire's tones. Part III is subtly dominated by a prosy voice somewhat like Defoe's. The dominant parody of Part IV is Kafka and his condensed tales of defeat and humiliation. The last section is also a parody of provincial autobiography, blurred with "real" autobiography, but Kafka's voice tends to reign. The sections, however, are not meagre or mechanically divided, and the witty parodies often have two sources: Eliot and Stevens' philosophical poems, for example, in Part I.

The initial phrase "These decibels" (RAM, 34) refers most unproblematically to the sound of the skaters as they skate, and the phrase "These decibels/ Are a kind of flagellation" (RAM, 34) refers to the sudden sound hitting the air. The only ambiguity here is the possibility that the "decibels" are meant to stand also for the poem itself being recited, since throughout the poem an analogy is made between the skaters, their infinite figure-eights and a circular poem, writing itself. One should also note that in this opening phrase Ashbery has purposely chosen a rather precious, Stevens-like vocabulary, a "philosophical" vocabulary, as a matter of fact, and one that is constantly being employed throughout the poem, which has for its chief theme the ecstasy of comprehension and incomprehension.

"An entity of sound/ Into which being enters, and is apart" (RAM, 34). This is one of the first paradoxes in a poem filled with paradox, and is the beginning of some ruthless meditations on observation itself. Ashbery meditates upon the relationship between the skaters and the sound they produce by skating; it is a thinly veiled comment on his own distance from his work. For, as we have noted, Ashbery is continuously meditating upon certain immediate scruples and problems, but at a distance. Ashbery can comment upon an immediate flower while giving the sensation that he is discussing a flower with no taste, no scent; the immediacy, however, is of "surface," language itself. In short, the author maintains his distance tactfully, with certain savage intrusions and self-dissolutions, all carefully framed.

"Their colors on a warm February day/ Make for masses of inertia" (RAM, 34). This passage suggests the skaters as they glide past, interestingly cast already in the language of art-criticism, one of the many vocabularies which Ashbery uses for parodic purposes and, in general, for dealing with observation in a somewhat dry, stereotyped manner which he derides while employing. The next phrase seems difficult but merely introduces a slight erotic presence of the skaters: "and hips/ Prod out of the violet-seeming into a new kind/ Of demand" (RAM, 34). In such guise does a certain outline take on sudden prominence in the *pointillist* vision of the poet, who is now considering certain aesthetic problems of "impressionism" and its demand for novel instantaneities: "Of demand that stumps the absolute because not new/ In the sense of the next one in an infinite series/ But, as it were, pre-existing or pre-seeming in/ Such a way as to contrast funnily with the unexpectedness/ And somehow push us all into perdition" (RAM, 34). The words "stumps" and "funnily" are appropriately inappropriate, Ashbery using them for the sudden colloquial force he needs to break out of a too-serious discussion of the question, "What makes *the skaters* significant?" Or another question seems to be asked, "What is it that makes the skaters skate?" This is the question, subtly, since it seems to be assumed in the later "The answer is that it is novelty/ That guides these swift blades o'er the ice" (RAM, 34). But the "new" demand is not new in the sense of a possible future ("the next one in an infinite series") but seems to the poet to have always been, which certainly does "contrast funnily" with unexpectedness and is, indeed, a paradox; a *déja vu* experience of "the new" itself, a Verlainesque sense of tedium, mixed with a puzzling sense of life's freshness. This is a paradox of the poem, which also ends with the eternal, and yet somehow always fresh, deranged "order" of the stars. This paradox is wittily said by the poet to "push us all into perdition." But the device seems pleasantly Zeno-esque. One thinks of Valéry calling out to the Eleatic master in "Cimitière Marin."

"The Skaters" is a poem of *porphyry* constantly admitting of layers of lucid moments of serene description. Thus, the next phrase: "Here a scarf flies, there an excited call is heard" (RAM, 34). The busy bucolic is thus part of the poem, the human scene that inspired the Callot prints Ashbery has a taste for,[2] those prints in which a great deal of wretchedness and energy are concentrated in excruciatingly small space. Throughout the introduction of the poem, the first person has been concealed and only the editorial "we" (in "push us all into perdition") has been used. Only in a slender sense are *we* all included. Later, the poem is to become a canvas of extreme solitude, a poem in which the *persona* is almost utterly isolated, with interiority reigning supreme, *no matter how fractured or imploded.*

A discussion of novelty then follows, and the theme of memory is introduced. "The human mind/ Cannot retain anything except perhaps the dismal two-note theme/ Of some sodden 'dump' or lament" (RAM, 34). The Elizabethan word "dump" serves to remind us of the great Shakespearean ruminations on ruin and the lack of stable monuments against mortality. There is erotic geniality in "We children are ashamed of our bodies/ But we laugh and, demanded, talk of sex again/ And all is well" (RAM, 34). This friendly and untroubled tone is immediately contrasted with the melancholy lament of "But how much survives? How much of any one of us survives?" (RAM, 34). This haunting question is dispersed immediately by a Whitmanesque and manic catalogue of stamps that are collected, and, curiously, "bright remarks"—a comic mixture of the gathering of the material and the mental. The catalogue ends with the extremely flat "One collects bullets. An Indianapolis, Indiana man collects slingshots of all epochs, and so on" (RAM, 34). Thus Ashbery maintains his Socratic poise, while asking the dignified "questions," however unanswerable.

As a matter of fact, answer is nearly impossible, and it is at this juncture that Ashbery plays an almost positivist or Wittgensteinian "game" on the "difficulty" of the question, or its *meaninglessness:* "Subtracted from our collections, though, these go on a little while, collecting aimlessly. We still support them" (RAM, 34). Through a pun, Ashbery demonstrates that even what the artist does not choose goes on choosing itself and, in a certain ambiguous sense, goes on choosing the artist, with a passivity which makes the question "What should I choose" (to collect, for example, or to use as a subject) absurd. It is at this point of extreme nonsensicality that Ashbery breaks up into explicit "Jabberwocky"-like violence and dream-wit. The "collection" is followed by an imaginary bestiary: "so little energy they have! And up the swollen sands/ Staggers the darkness fiend, with the storm fiend close behind him!" (RAM, 34). The storm and darkness *motifs* will return in this poem, but here what is most significant is that the question has been followed to its positivist conclusion of dissolution, rather than solution. Compromise has been made, the question vitiated, but it is followed by an explosive dream image repeated many times throughout the poem, as if to say, "This game is over," a sweeping of the men off the chess board.

Another example of this renunciation of the rhetorical question is the explicit "house of cards collapsing" image used to stop part of a discussion on poetic explanation and meaning itself, ending: "But am afraid I'll/ Be of no help to you. Goodbye" (RAM, 40). Ashbery here relates causality to the discussion of meaning, since the causality discussed is that which gave a certain coherence to supposed "nineteenth century poetics" in the view of the *persona* at this point. We should be careful not too easily to ascribe any "opinions" to *Ashbery*, who prefers a shifting aesthetic and presence. "I simply wanted to see how many opinions I had about everything," he said once in a private interview, concerning "The Skaters' " deposition about Schubert: "I love Schubert actually."[3] But Humpty-Dumpty will have it all ways.

The next part of the poem, "True, melodious tolling does go on in that awful pandemonium" (RAM, 35) contrasts (in the by now expected unexpectedness of Ashbery) with the quiet beginning of the poem. It is a catalogue of grotesque musical effects, partially patterned on John Cage's prepared piano pieces, which influenced Ashbery as a "permission" toward aleatory techniques, and also toward the enucleation of "the everyday" in his early *collage* pieces. This passage is filled with the paradox that noise, too, is also and always a species of music: "tuba notes awash on the great flood, ruptures of xylophone, violins, limpets, grace-notes, the musical instrument called serpent, viola da gambas, aeolian harps, clavicles, pinball machines, electric drills, que sais-je encore?" (RAM, 35). As in Whitman, this catalogue is carefully modulated, first the rather *overwritten* sentimentalized tubas "awash" on the great flood; next the jazzy percussion of xylophone with the funnily "literary" noun "ruptures," followed by the classical and rather common violins, immediately followed by limpets, which the *OED* defines as "a gasteropod mollusc of the genus Patella." This nonmusical, nonsensical *instrument* is followed by grace-notes, which are the musical embellishments, here almost last and least substantial of all, a veritable deliquescence. Next in the catalogue comes "the musical instrument called serpent," which is defined by *OED* as "an obsolete bass wind instrument of deep tone, about 8 feet long, made of wood covered with leather . . . Thackerary refers to 'the bellowing and braying of the serpents' " (*OED*) and certainly it is paradigmatic of Ashbery to use this *Borgesian schol- arship* and "to dredge up" the obsolete instrument which was primarily used for military bands. Next in the series comes viola da gambas and aeolian harps, a strange juxtaposition of archaic instruments, active and passive, but the following is more truly *absurd:* clavicles, pinball machines, electric drills, and the sud- den gallicism: "que sais-je encore?" (RAM, 35).

What makes this "nonsense" catalogue truly dramatic is that the absurdity of its description is matched by the realism in which it depicts the electric Ashberyan-Cagean method of em- ploying *all* that can be *given*. As a matter of fact, the poet says, "The performance has rapidly reached your ear," another of the insistences upon the "action poem" quality of "The Skaters," as the poem "unfolds" before us simultaneously with a composi- tion, no matter how rococo, embellished with clavicles(!), a seemingly un-notated music. The "reader" is made to stand within the poem and is evoked: "silent and tear-stained, in the post-mortem shock, you stand listening, awash/ With memories of hair in particular, part of the welling that is you." This "you" is also the *persona* addressing himself. This is followed by yet another comical catalogued "gurgling of harp," surely a Lewis Carroll-like "nonsensical" description of harp sound. Particularly amusing is the effect of having a metronome, in this most disor- derly of catalogues, be the final "instrument" listed.

Lucid indifference, now, is described as the poet's "stock response." "And still no presentiment, no feeling of pain before or after./ The passage sustains, does not give" (RAM, 35). The metrical sense of closure to this paragraph is significant. Throughout the poem, Ashbery has to deal with the problem of such a disorderly "long poem" and exactly how to "sustain" it, without "giving" too much, too fast or too easily. He proceeds by carefully unfolding his motifs, and keeping the opening para- graphs cautiously curtailed and suspenseful. The poet always reserves his landscape observation, meditations upon "the skaters," phenomenology of a most subtle sort, as a continuous "music." The smaller curves of the lyrics within, however, are sufficiently delimited. A poem of many parts, "The Skaters" *demands* its length and its many mocking closures.

The next passage in "The Skaters" is a pathetic meditation on personal weakness, a parody of classic Chinese stories of failure, recounted and ironically framed, with sufficient *repoussoir*, leading to an indictment of the *persona*. "Yet to go from 'not interesting' to 'old and uninteresting' " (RAM, 35) is a bitter reminder, like Eliot's "aged eagle," of spiritual sinful despair and must be taken seriously throughout Ashbery's poem, though with the reminder that (1) this is also a vestige of the palpable injustices dealt to an explicitly solitary figure, a self-proclaimed passive person and probably being cast here as the experimentalist who writes these difficult lines and that (2) the despair, like that of the "aged eagle" in Eliot, is merely one moment in the poem and must be seen as the preparation for the moments of greater "ontological happiness," if not "security." Ashbery celebrates disequilibria.

Ellipses always serve to modulate toward strange colloquialisms, such as "To hear the wings of the spirit, though far. . . ." (a taste, by the way, of Ashbery's later use of devotional clichés, which becomes rampant in *Three Poems*, particularly "The New Spirit" and "The System") ". . . Why do I hurriedly undrown myself to cut you down?" The modulation from self-vindication to loathing threatens to make the poem a series of humiliations for the reader's expectation, explicitly in the passage containing the exclamatory outburst, "I'd like to bugger you all up" or "you remind me of a lummox I used to know," which reminds one of Michaux's equally sudden savagery. Modern poetry is a series of insults to the speeding reader. In "The Skaters" Ashbery transcends Michaux's bitterness by the extreme mannerist "reaching out" to denounce his readership. "Present demands" are again stated, however, in a way that reflects "badly" upon the author, and a Rimbaldien regret is voiced concerning the estrangement of the ego: "And I have a dim intuition that I am that other 'I' with which we began" (RAM, 35). Again, this *dérèglement* of the "I" is cast in terms of *time,* and like the sequence of the first stanza, novelty is contrasted with the eternal, and here, moreover, with the more embittering facts of the persona's middle age.

Age is throughout the poem one of the new grim binary oppositions to the theme of aesthetic novelty. The lines, as in Shakespearean sonnets, seem ever fresh while the author's yellow leaves or few or none are noted. "Tears"—one of the usual images of romantic configurations in *skenas* of suffering—are conjured up once again, only to be followed by a blank and yet still Rilkesque and grim couplet concerning this mortality: "The evidence of the visual henceforth replaced/ By the great shadow of trees falling over life" (RAM, 35). This couplet however is comical when one sees that (1) it is a rather odd couplet in diction, the drab "evidence" and "henceforth" contrasting funnily with the shadow of the trees and (2) it is all a joke in which the quiet meditation upon data, visual data, the data of the skaters, is replaced by nothing less than a *catastrophe,* or at least the shadow of a catastrophe, the emergency of "the great shadow of trees falling over life" (RAM, 35). The following couplet is even more ironic and truncated: "A child's devotion/ To this normal, shapeless entity . . . ." The word *entity* reminds us at once of *the entity of sound* at the poem's beginning, which was demanding the author's devotion, and the entity of the shadow of trees, but the adjective "normal" seems rather uncanny here. An ellipsis follows, which leaves one with the almost sentimental sense of impending doom, but following that is the genial: "Forgotten as the words fly briskly across," another "action phrase" denoting the poem's composition in present time. Meaning is associated with a species of *grace* in this poem, with the infinite and ethereal figure-eight, and with snow, and here we have the first antinomian image and explicit figure of "natural" *meaning:* "Bringing down meaning as snow from a low sky, or rabbits flushed from a wood" (RAM, 35–36). Meaning covers and is uncovered, ever not quite.

The next passage, concerning meaning again, is most ambiguous and filled explicitly with parodox: "How strange that the narrow perspective lines/ Always seem to meet, although parallel, and that an insane ghost could do this" (RAM, 36). On the one hand, Ashbery seems to be commenting on paradox in an art critical language as if vision itself were being ruminated upon, and yet what we finally gather is that the looming up of the past as by a haunting phantasm is the subject, with a kind of Breughelesque image of landscape in childhood: "the horse, dragging the sledge of a perspective line./ Dim banners in the distance, to die. . . . And nothing put to rights. The pigs in their cages// And so much snow" (RAM, 36). Ashbery's childhood is seen as detritus, "waste and ashes," but fecund mulch as it were, "so that cathedrals may grow" (RAM, 36).

In the beginning were language and meaning, childish and the only things we have. The snow is not only the snow of evocation and childhood scenes, the farmyard perhaps where Ashbery lived as a child, but also the February snow of the present time of the poem. The dismal but hilarious hint "Spring with its promise of winter" (RAM, 36) is made to remind us once again that any burgeoning in the poem only foreshadows utter annihilation. The horse is now used like one of Eliot's gentle figures of suffering, "And the horse nears them and weeps" (RAM, 36). Ashbery makes this all the more wretched by distributing parsimoniously his "symbols of misery" so that the evocation of the sea "felt behind oak wands, noiselessly pouring" (RAM, 36), with its marvelous freshness and grace, is all the more menaced by the dismal, Daumier-like horror of the weeping horse. The dragging and weeping horse is also a most horrifying binary opposition to the graceful human artist, and yet begins in his weeping to be like the artist, after all, in the mood of *dump* or lament. An artist is just a suffering animal on skates: a sustained joke.

The next passage tends to be quite lucid and matter-of-fact, and is a fine modulation after the rather mottled and difficult passage concerning perspective and misery. It is also concerned with misery, but now in a first-person that is readily recognizable as a parody of an epistolary "I." "So much has passed through my mind this morning" (RAM, 36). The author is still placed in the February landscape, with a brief mention of snow, which consistently falls through the poem, but is now writing to a more or less recognizable "you," as beloved or friend. But the news is foreboding: "Sometimes the interval/ Of bad news is so brisk that . . ." (RAM, 36). This complaint is often raised in various ways in the poems, a Lucretian "Sweet it is to watch other men's ships sink," and is echoed explicitly in Ashbery's complaint that the human body can be hurt in so many ways that it is difficult to know where to turn. As a matter of fact, the theme of meaninglessness throughout the poem, or difficulty of comprehension, is made all the more excruciating by three demands the author is making: (1) demands for aesthetic novelty, freshness, and adventure, (2) demand that man's extreme vulnerability somehow be justified, (3) demand that something be a consolation in this immense solitude, if not a beloved, then *something*. But in most cases, the breakdown of *logos*, the positivist response, the Wittgensteinian silence is echoed in "The very reaction's puny" (RAM, 36), though the poet actually gives *the poem* as his response and theodicy, and character armor, one might add, against all vulnerability. "Mild effects" and "puny reactions" are the very stuff, the pleasure of this labyrinthine fantasy. But the peaceful, self-reflexive poem is very strong and made to last.

The next "paragraph" or stanza is antinomian, in the sense that it refers to the breakdown of the moral order under the reign of grace. The surrealist poet sees the "great wind" of faith and grace cleansing and sweeping into the future, and the older order receives its first of many rebukes: "Everything is trash!" (RAM, 37). The new order can be seen as the principle of no principle, an unprogrammatic programme that reigns over this poem to its very conclusion, in which the stars of Taurus, Leo, and Gemini are said to "rise in perfect order," except that ironically this order refers to no particular season and place, but "merely" to the poetic order[4] in which the words "sounded correct." The moral order of Kant, in which reason finds its antinomy naturally, its contradiction, is savagely imaged in this last configuration of stars that point *to no exterior reality.* The poet, therefore, is forced throughout to praise the intensity of his own "minor acts," that mildly result from *poesis,* likened to the Sisyphean, infinitely graceful, infinitely circular acts of Skaters, who "elaborate their distances" (RAM, 37). The variations of the Skaters themselves are said to be variations on "the exquisite theme" (RAM, 37), the theme which we see to be *the breakdown of the old order,* symbolized in Eliotic "dried grasses" (RAM, 37), and the concomitant antinomian and surrealist rule of grace, in which only *poesis* itself is a saving principle for the poet, a consolation not of Boethian reason but of *the exquisite poem.* This is the theme of art not merely for the sake of art, but a difficult species of salvation. A redemptive Chinese box, as later seen in "The Recital," is the novelty and adventure that affords the poet his one relation, that of the hermetic voice crying in the slovenly wilderness to contact the audience streaming from the empty hall (TP, 118). "The Skaters" has a *persona* of extreme desolation and solipsism, but here too the poem itself, and its image of a mild sport of some struggle, becomes its own support.

"[T]here is error/ In so much precision" (RAM, 38), Ashbery says, paraphrasing Aristotle's famous remark that every field has its own degree of precision. Ashbery here is making a defense of artifice, defending immediately the glamorous artificiality of his vocabulary, which avoids the demotic except in juxtapositions of ironical effect. Modern poetry is not so much Wordsworthian live speech as it is a lively dead language meant to haunt ghosts. Ashbery attempts a summation, only to undercut, of course, the idea of summation: "It is time now for a general understanding of/ The meaning of all this" (RAM, 38). This passage makes it obvious that the poet is tolerant of discontinuity and the loss of *logos*, and is intolerant of and savagely parodies the idea of a static understanding and certainty. Keats criticized the poet who like the consecutive thinker must resolve into certainties, and in our own day in physics Heisenberg has utilized probability to underline the "Uncertainty Principle" with some explanatory power. Ashbery refuses certainty in his parody-image of "explanation." The poem cannot be padded out with the discursive, in any sense of certainty and coherence. The problem of his poem, he states by way of paradox, is to be its own destroyer. Like Rauschenberg, who erased a de Kooning drawing in an extreme betrayal of the old order, Ashbery takes self-laceration to the extreme, in which the poem itself creates its own "bitter impression of absence" (RAM, 39). For Ashbery the theme of absence, with all the negative corollaries and connotations—love's lost paradise, *deus absconditus*, the absence of law, the loss of childhood, loss of memory—is so fundamental that it receives a funny fetishistic reification in the lines: "Nevertheless these are fundamental absences, struggling to get up and be off themselves" (RAM, 39).

The exquisite poem is then likened to falling snow ("this poem/ Which is in the form of falling snow" [RAM, 39]) in an extraordinary simile which does become a self-description. Self-reference is one of the logical difficulties with which Lewis Carroll struggled in symbolic logic and with which he created some most dazzling paradoxes, still to be resolved. Self-reference is what many art critics claim "collage" has for theme, and much else of twentieth-century art, in its constant pointing to its own flatness (in the case of the picture plane) and to its materiality (for example, in paintings which utilize the back and front as surface, whereas Renaissance "rules" had maintained paintings merely contained the "front" as surface). Ashbery's poem, in this passage, is seen to be valuable not merely in its discrete moments, which would make it an epic of lyric moments as described by Poe. Nor is it attempting a kind of resolution or "truism" and "whole." The poem's value is in its "rhythm of the series of repeated jumps, from/ abstract into positive and back to a slightly less/ diluted abstract" (RAM, 39). The procedure here is that of manneristic self-reference and *repoussoir*. "Mild effects" resulting from this procedure are merely a humiliating judgment of the poet, but he is at least giving us an insight into his conception of the modest structural resources of the poem. The discrete leaps of the sections explicitly designate the poem as one of discontinuity. The denial of any "importance of the whole impression of the storm" (RAM, 39) reminds us that the poem is not striving for classical unified and coherent composition. Coherence may be parodied, as it is in this long Virgilian simile, but the "wistful parody" that coherence has become means that incoherence threatens to become the immoralist's rule of rejection. As a matter of fact, the poem should not be, and cannot be with any "precision," studied as an exercise in structural unity, except in the paradoxical sense that it is unified by its theme and style of disunity and fragmentation.

An argument concerning "The Waste Land" might run along the same lines. The text as it now stands is either a highly unified composition, or merely an *exercis du style* in a high form of Rimbaud's self-scattering. There is an ironical problem in that the original text of "The Waste Land" shows greater coherence, and that Pound, the "miglior fabbro," resolutely cut for great resilience and intensity, but also towards a technique of *montage* and *juxtaposition* in which the older coherency is more poignantly lost than in Eliot's original version. Surely Eliot himself never went any further in dissociational techniques, which Pound (see "Pisan Cantos") certainly proceeded to effect.

The discussion of the older order of causality is a fundamental part of "The Skaters." "Romantic" causality is deposed as a plain old-fashioned order, but the new order also suffers from seeming "phony": an artificial paradise. As a matter of fact, both orders seem ironically difficult to sustain. The world "of Schubert's lieder" (RAM, 40) with its coherency, say, of sonata form, is deposed as a "mismanaged mess" (RAM, 40). The poet himself erases his own *persona* in a sudden colloquial goodbye, reminding us of the theme of a disappearing, jovially ruthless Humpty-Dumpty in Ashbery's poetry. The fragmentation is extreme; the poet has wandered into a wonderland of new causalities and incoherences, but no one stands as an illuminator of the problem. The rule of *agape* is far from the solipsistic uncertainties of the poet; normative relations are deranged in style and drama, and deranged similes apply: "As balloons are to the poet, so to the ground/ Its varied assortment of trees. The more assorted they are, the/ Vaster his experience" (RAM, 40). Here the "they" has returned to the balloons, in a dangling, almost nongrammatical maneuver, and the balloons are also degraded: "Strung up there for publicity purposes" (RAM, 40) in a commercial quotidian. The poet is employing images of transiency and risk, and suddenly, after observing children's bubbles, he exclaims, in another self-reference: "Where was I?" (RAM, 40), returning only then to the extended balloon image. For the poet only "profane illumination," or the confession of its lack, suffices.

The balloons, in their image of drift, are also aspects of an existence slightly less weighed down by the gravities of anxiety, and their relationship to the land is anomalous, "not exactly commenting on it" (RAM, 40), like the reticent poet. The poet does not merely conceal himself within or behind trees, like a hamadryad, but he may use the balloon as a vehicle, though there is a pun on the wise passivity of this vehicle "letting the balloons/ Idle him out of existence, as a car idles" (RAM, 40). The idle poet is now "traveling faster" (RAM, 40), and in a glamorous demotic existence is said to be "belted into the night." The image however is not solely one of satisfied wishes and hedonistic lack of legalism, for now the wish is simply to be "more and more . . . unlike someone" (RAM, 40). The poet is "stuck in the world" as Hamlet in his nutshell, and the "system" and the coherence of the system is as hermetically sealed as his own labyrinths. The poet is then viewed with Hamletesque disdain: "a half-man" (RAM, 40). And the "pump" *leitmotif*, that will appear in the termination of the poem, is now employed. This is an Eliotic figure, a *symboliste* resource, reminding us that the wells and resources of tradition are frozen or dried out. This is also emphasized by the sullen intrusion of "No Skating" (RAM, 40), reminding us of the later: "And so their comment is: 'No Comment' " in *The Double Dream of Spring*'s lyric "John Clare" (p. 36).

The first section of the poem ends with a *repoussoir*, "to hold the candle up to the album" (RAM, 41), as the poet examines his own lament: "Placed squarely in front of his dilemma." The alternatives are said to be "unsmiling" (RAM, 40). The old order of fashionable continuity has been shattered, as cubism shattered even further the fruit-dish of Cézanne, and the poet has not yet seen any possibility of *synthesis*. The dilemma, then, is the drying up or freezing out of the older principles, now paraded and parodied mercilessly, and yet, within this hurry, as in "time control" in a chess of life, the poet in an emergency attempts to end his poem not in a lament but in affirmation.

There are four major movements to "The Skaters," not exactly from "abstract to positive and back to a slightly less diluted abstract," but to some extent, in sonata form, from a discussion of the skaters and their relationship to the poet's dilemma of uncertainty, to a second movement of possibilities of dream and vision. The third movement emerges with parodies of a Lucretian naturalism and images of the normative world, and the fourth movement ends the labyrinth with parodies of negativism and failure, ending with a stoical affirmation of the process of *poesis* itself and Marcus Aurelius-like endurance. The last movement is in some senses more pulverized, more fractured than the others, comparable to the sudden flurries of parodies in the last section of "The Waste Land," but it is also here that the affirmative nature of parody becomes most evident, as a cohesive principle in *paradox* and discontinuity, somehow becoming the humorous homogeneous tone of this most heterogeneous world. Probability is thus seen to be applied throughout the poem as a topic, in the uncertainty of an "exquisite theme." The distantiation and reticence of the *persona*, in his risks and solipsisms, in his dream world and its vulnerability, are never dissolved. The poem, like "The New Spirit" and "The Recital," goes perhaps "over" what Christians would describe as an "abyss" and "the conversion threshold," but it remains still the poem of the unconverted, profane immoralist.

The second section begins, ironically enough, with a sentence fragment reminding one of normative disruptions, say in the post office: "Under the window marked 'General Delivery' "

(RAM, 41). *Personism* was Frank O'Hara's term for a poem which tried to mimic the epistolary mode; and Ashbery begins for a moment to think of this as a possible alternative. "This should be a letter" (RAM, 41), but this letter would be meant not to affirm the relations of the poet and reader but to disrupt the equilibrium of the reader: "Throwing you a minute to one side" (RAM, 41). Here poetry is not a letter; language is not a pencil.

A letter seems comparable to the lyric mode, its "sadness small and appreciable" (RAM, 41). The poem does indeed accumulate, as Poe stated, the lyric intensities which may be a long poem's only way of succeeding, but Ashbery has rejected, in the previous section, this possibility of value in the "mere flakes" as in a small sadness of perishable pleasures or "bubbles." The horror of his situation of uncertainty ends in another disruptive apostrophe: "I'd like to bugger you all up./ Deliberately falsify all your old suck-ass notions/ Of how chivalry is being lived. What goes on in beehives" (RAM, 41–42). Again, the order that is attacked, including now a political-sexual and sociological lament, is seen to be the messy old order, perhaps with its Darwinian explanations or its religious pieties. Ashbery, unlike an Albert Einstein or Bertrand Russell, does not use logic for any pietistic purpose. The paragraph ends with extreme doubt and uncertainty, the solipsistic doubt raised yet again, and without question marks: "How much of any one person is there" (RAM, 42). This is the corollary to the Heraclitean paradox of flux. The poet is not merely a static other, nor yet another, like a river, in eternal flux. He is merely a figure, as described in the modulations of the skaters, always in a new position on a "thin ice" of uncertainty, if one may employ this trope, and he experiences feelings that Freud called those of "unreality," not the Eliotic "unreal City," but the self-dissolution in which interiority itself is threatened. The poet here seems affectless and cold, the propositions are laid down in drab sentence fragments, that mock the poem's earlier exquisite manner. Torpor and despair are here mimicked in the flat tones of the poem. The two-dimensionalism of the diction accurately reflects the theme of "the horror and the boredom," when the glory is all absented. One does not cross the same poem even once.

The poet's solution is to return "under the eaves" in a gesture of hermeticism. The "incoherencies" of the poet are likened to "the incoherencies of day [which] melt in/ A general wishful thinking of night" (RAM, 42). The binary opposition of fundamental day, with its normative relations now insupportable to the poet, and night, with its automatisms that result in associational streams that can never be fulfilled, is here dramatically deployed. The old order is mocked in the explicitly antipietistic: "Old heavens, you used to tweak above us" (RAM, 42). Here the sky and the heavens are colloquially used interchangeably, but surely the connotations of the sacred space are degraded by the casual transposition.

The poet is now said to be "parodying" the heavens themselves, "Your invisible denials" (RAM, 42). Just as the *hidden god* is seen to be frustrating the poet with absence, discontinuity, and despair, so the poem is taken as a black mirror between realities. "I call to you there, but I do not think that you will answer me" (RAM, 42). The Hindus have a system of "neti neti" (not this, not this) in which the *negative way* is outlined by the proposition that no adjective can be applied to the *Atman*. Ashbery, too, utilizes the *asimilar negative way* to hold up a blank image which accurately displays the *tedium vitae* of "this tedious planet, earth" (RAM, 43).

The antipietistic mode is also employed in: "you seem to have abandoned them [i.e., storms] in favor of endless light./ I cannot say that I think the change much of an improvement"

(RAM, 43). The binary opposition of darkness and light is seen by Ashbery to be dissolved; the extreme of ambiguity is reached. The poet is taking a position somewhat analogous to the antinomian "beyond good and evil" of Nietzsche and Blake, but he has yet to announce any illuminating coherencies of his new position. The poem continues to a "L'Invitation au voyage" suddenly picked up *in media res*. "We are nearing the Moorish coast" (RAM, 43). Transitions, as always, are startling if controlled. Such are the nomadic moves in a truth-less world of metaphor and metonymy.

Ashbery's *Voyage* is a dream voyage of (unfulfilled) fantasies and represents a possible "alternative" at this point of the poem. It is one of the sensuous illusions with which the poet concerns himself. The quatrains are delicately arranged in Whitmanesque long lines of up to ten feet. The poet describes an earthly paradise, and gives up the normative existence of "office desks, radiators" (RAM, 44). The departure for the earthly paradise is described in Kafkaesque self-ridicule: "hurry before the window slams down" (RAM, 44). The nonsense confusions are hilariously described: "the boats are really boats this time" (RAM, 44). The train may be a boat train, but the boats are boats, thus at least some tautologies give the poet instant certainties, only to dissolve yet again: "This continual changing back and forth?" (RAM, 44). The rigor of pietistic laments does not appeal to the poet, and he shouts his negative to the heavens ("No! I'll not accept that any more, you bewhiskered old caverns of blue" [RAM, 44]) and he screams for his right to graceful hedonism and the order of grace: "I shall never forget this moment// Because it consists of purest ecstasy" (RAM, 44). Here the long emjambment, working between stanzas, permits the poet to employ the longest "bars of rest" as an ecstatic silence to entrance the reader, just as the poet is entranced during the dream voyage. The caesura wanders now quickly: "It is all passing! It is past! No, I am here" (RAM, 45), and the syn-copations quickly reassert the dynamism and perishability of pleasure within the dream. Such is the poet's critique of any easy exoticism.

The dream may be the "happiest" but the sudden stops and starts apply a certain dismal juxtaposition to the theme of wish fulfillment. Just as day and night are ambiguities, so dream and nightmare here modulate incessantly. Swamps and rainy weather beset the poet, and comically full hotels. The waters cannot support the economically fundamental fish. The stormy scene changes, after a brief interlude in which a wedding is parodied, and the ship starts again. The uncertainties of the fantasy-voyage are analogous to the theme of uncertainty deployed throughout the poem. Rimbaud's Drunken Boat is pretty damaged, by now. The poet, like the comic hero in Buster Keaton movies, is always capable of making it in "just time enough." The speed is variegated and lacks dignity, as in the demotic catalogue: "Pulling, tugging us along with them . . ./ Golden and silver confetti" (RAM, 46). This is paradigmatic of the "nuptial quality of [JA's] verses (he is always marrying the whole world),"[5] for as in this O'Hara quotation, we see a poetry that loves to digest the whole world, which is now seen as "a motley and happy crowd" (RAM, 46) all voyaging with the poet, who now excludes none. A certain normative relation but with a motley multitude is resumed, "And full of laughter and tears, we sidle once again with the other passengers" (RAM, 46) but we are reminded, as at the beginning of the voyage, that the poet is travelling in the direction where none are free. The unknown of Baudelaire is parodied in a triple ejaculatory sentence that effectively demoralizes or punctures it: "Into the unknown, the unknown that loves us, the great unknown!" (RAM, 46). Ashbery's poetry is now a bittersweet criticism of orthodox symbolism.

Immediately after this quatrain, the voyage dissolves mercilessly and an image of descent is used with extreme and dismay-
ing disjunction: "So man nightly/ Sparingly descends" (RAM,
46). The poet announces that the dream is over in the most
subtle sense; the adverb *nightly* gives us a disturbing sense of
the inevitability of dream and illusion. "The pumps" are now
said to be working, but in a crazily named distance: "Gannos-
fonadiga" (RAM, 47). And the stars are summoned up only in
drifting, widely spaced sentence fragments ("slow-imagined
stars" [RAM, 47,]) all combining in an orchestrated dissatisfaction. The poet is slowly modulating from a lyric mode to
another discursive passage, perhaps what in the "snowflake"
passage is said to be "positive," though these "discursive" passages are in another sense also abstract and critical.

The skaters are brought back at this moment of the dissolution of the Rimbaldien and Baudelairesque drunken voyage.
The "figure eight" is seen to be an image of "the freedom to be
gained in this kind of activity" (RAM, 47). Ashbery's demotic
use of "kind of," which becomes an aesthetic stammer in the
late prose poems of *Three Poems*, is here used to indicate the
self-referentiality of the poem. The poem is also compared to
certain paintings, and the humble principle now invoked is that
of "limitations imposed" (RAM, 47). That is, a rule of conscience
in aesthetic matters at least is seen to be one alternative of the
chaotic *ethos* and *mythos* of the erotic daydreaming of the poet.
A "kind of rhythm substituting for 'meaning' " is an extremely
opaque figure, which reminds one of the snow-passage, here culminating in the sense that *intellectual-musical activity somehow
can and must substitute for principled, discursive purpose*, particularly in the light of "the problem of death and survival" and
pain (RAM, 48). There is a curious juxtaposition of the literary
and colloquial in this proposition of suffering: "Scarcely we
know where to turn to avoid suffering. I mean/ There are so

many places." An image of horror and blankness is seen in this "discursive definition" concerning visual perspective. The "vanishing point" is funnily enough the place where lines "meet" (RAM, 48). So, in Ashbery, the perspective seems to vanish and the possibility of normative love (normative as, say, Kitty and Levin in Tolstoy's *Anna Karenina*) is here disrupted. The question of poverty is also raised in "pop" images of misery: "Rusted tomato can" (RAM, 48). We are reminded that even the description of "real" poverty is unreal, literary illusion: "All this, wedged into a pyramidal ray of light, is my own invention" (RAM, 48). There is a brief joke against American pragmatism while Ashbery parodies the Horatio Alger formula: how to use the tomato can to "[make] a fortune" (RAM, 49). Interestingly, the American ingenuity here described is very close to the labyrinthine ingenuities of the poet. But commercialism in the poem is always seen as opposed to the *absurd*, as the stupidities of Flaubert's bourgeois commercialists to the dreamy Emma. Ashbery, like Warhol, is a subtle critic of the commercial world, and his so-called success does not indicate comprehension of that critique.

Another "ingenious" paragraph in "The Skaters" is the alchemical description of a "flame fountain" (RAM, 49). A menu is served up, very much in the sense of Williams' collages in *Paterson* or O'Hara's "real" menu in "Biotherm,"[6] an idiotic but real "texture" that the poet finds touching and humorous and that is a fundamental echo of the theme of illusion. The poet is now in a didactic role, but of the least importance: "Add gradually one ounce" (RAM, 49). The journalistic tone is now one of chemical cookbooks, vapid yet precise, and the image is portentous, and truly arising, like the quintessence, *ab nihilo:* "The whole surface of the liquid will become luminous" (RAM, 49). The poet interjects a diffident datum: "Sure, but a simple shelter from this or other phenomena is easily contrived"

(RAM, 49). Here the chemical cookbook's *caveat* and advice is parodied into an enormous dictum concerning the possibilities of defenses against one's own Faustian predicaments. The poem proceeds to a spectacular description of the spectacle in long Whitmanesque lines: "Its sparks seem to aspire to reach the sky!" (RAM, 49). Transient bubbles are now seen as revitalized and Promethean. The colloquial "Great balls of fire" is the precise description of this "managed mess." "Invisible writing" is then immediately described in banal propositions, but the reader remembers that this image of a zero degree of substantiality in literature is the "fundamental absence" of which the poem concerns itself.

The "fire-fountain" is still imaged as continuing, but just like the dream voyage, it is a central image of sputtering uncertainty. The dream ends in the bitter disillusionment of day; and Faustian gnosticism and alchemy end in "a hellish stink and wild fumes of pitch/ Acrid as jealousy" (RAM, 50). The last phrase is particularly masterful in its alignment of the odor and the abstract, that slightly "less diluted abstract" (one thinks of "malignant and turbaned Turk") with which Ashbery achieves his most metaphysically witty effects. "That side is closed" is another *caveat* parodying the chemistry book; a vapid didacticism here employed as the only available means of poetical pedagogy. The fountain is now subsiding, but the activity is pejoratively and summarily deposed as "insane" (RAM, 50). Spring is juxtaposed against the "hellish stink," spring with its own promise, somewhat more natural than the alchemy previously described. After the collagiste ironies of the fire-writing, Ashbery surrenders to an image, however clichéd and lacerated, of "a young boy and girl leaning against a bicycle" (RAM, 50). The image shows its irony in the lamppost which disappears into a tree, whose leaves are said to "suffocate" the lamppost.

Once again his vanishing points have their hideous aspects glaringly revealed.

The irony of normative life is given a comical, Chaplinesque image, a "wan ending" of "humiliation and defeat" ("Rivers and Mountains," RAM, 10) in the mailman's first day on a new job, meeting up with the "hideous bulldog" (RAM, 50). The bulldog's eyes are also "hellish," but this image is hysterically dissolved to an erotic scene of a woman engaged in attending to her stockings, while a "chap with a hat" is walking into the eternally waiting catastrophe. Here the *coup de grace* is given by "a speeding hackney cabriolet" (RAM, 51). "This is a puzzle scene" (RAM, 51), says Ashbery, "worthy of the poet's pen," and yet he dissolves this notion in the comical idea that it is only an illusion created by the "fire demon." The spring scene is suddenly seen to be, like an endless poem about shadows in ink wells, a parenthesis concerning the images on a "dubious surface." So, we the readers have been tricked by this spring passage. The postman, the cabriolet, the white night, are all dissolved on the "dubious surface" of the fountain. But one can learn to tolerate these illusions. *Agape* is not being brought up here, but aesthetic appreciation, in Ashbery's funny aesthetic use of the degraded notion of love: "But love can appreciate it,/ Use or misuse it for its own ends. Love is stronger than fire" (RAM, 51). The joke is that aesthetic appreciation may learn pragmatically to enjoy the meaningless or disjunct illusions presented by the "phosphorescent fountain."

And the "proof" of appreciation is that Ashbery ends Part II of "The Skaters" not in a slight dilution but in the complete Prospero-like dissolution of the "heaving . . . fountain." The "wan ending" is here the paling of the fountain, but the "lovers remain fixed, as if permanently, on the air of the lab" (RAM, 51). The ironical "as if" is underlined by emphasis of the sudden

Heraclitean flux: "Not for long though. And now they too collapse" (RAM, 51). The theme of Part II of "The Skaters" may
remind us of Rilke in the eighth "Duino Elegy": "It fills us. We
arrange it. It decays. We rearrange it, and decay ourselves."[7]
The poet's vision "too fades away" but as of now the poet himself has not collapsed, as we will see him collapse in pratfalls
and ritual defeats several times before the end of Part IV of the
waste land of "The Skaters." As Part I introduced us to the aesthetic methodology of discontinuity, Part II has seemingly exhausted all the resources of dream and the alchemy of dream.
Even the aesthetic "fire-fountain" has faded as resource and "invisible writing" of childhood. The poem has ended again with a
"bitter impression of absence."

Ashbery erupts at the beginning of Part III, suddenly, against
the "you" of the poem: "you/ Remind me of some lummox I
used to know" (RAM, 51). The poet plays Lewis Carroll's jovial
but ruthless Humpty-Dumpty and the reader plays a bewil-
dered Alice. The "meaninglessness" of the poem is not merely
what bewilders *the poet,* but is also part of his threatening arse-
nal *against* the *bétises* of the reader looking for too easy coherencies. This reminds one of an Eliotic "complexity" possibly
necessary and fruitful at stages of civilization's own complexity
or decadence. Ashbery's parodies are simple, his topics and
themes are recurrent and not overly perplexing, but where the
knot is ravelled, he refuses to unravel it poetically into neo-
Georgian pieties. "Understand?" he suddenly interrogates,
though the preceding opacity is particularly inscrutable, and
manneristically concerns a "secret." "Here comes the answer: is
it because apples grow/ On the tree, or because it is green?"
(RAM, 52). The answer is here parodied as a question and the
Lewis Carroll paradox is viciously portrayed, for even the question is impossible to understand. Positivism's work is a logical
analysis of the species of questions which can be said to be an-

swerable. Ashbery's questions are palpably unanswerable, but just as many positivists found all answerable questions were finally trivial and "naturalistic," so Ashbery's questions resonate like the illusory dream fountain and become, after all, "this banality which in the last analysis is our/ Most precious possession" ("French Poems," DDS, 39). The poet dissolves into bleak dream fragments ("If I should . . . If I said you were there/ The . . . towering peace around us might/ Hold up the way it breaks" [RAM, 52]). Possibilities end in disruptions, and what follows is a dismal *catalogue raisonné* of horror.

Paradox in Ashbery is used for effects not dissimilar to what orthodoxy praises concerning the jokes and parables of Jesus. They are colloquial antinomies pointing out unusual departures from common sense interpretation: "Only one thing exists: the fear of death" (RAM, 52). The only certainty, says Ashbery, is perpetual uncertainty and the root *uncertainty* is that of certain death. This is a central passage of Ashbery, who, like O'Hara, rejects all deism and immortality in his poems, even for aesthetic visions, which may "hang" (as in "The Skaters'" firefountain or "The Recital's" poem-song) but finally and naturalistically fade. The vanishing point *is* the end, and the poet lacks all the confidence that any public poet of antiquity might be said to have had. The poet has not escaped from his early despair in the least and here gives a positive version of it: "What I said first goes: sleep, death and hollyhocks" (RAM, 53). Just as in the *agon* of Eliot's "birth, copulation, and death," Ashbery's despair is delivered in rhythms of doggerel and *Americana*. And the poet also enters a plea once more against pieties of the old "cause-and-effect" of romatic impressions of coherency and immortality: "But no dramatic arguments for survival, and please/ no magic justification of results" (RAM, 53). William James' Christian Science and will to believe do not enter here, *just a will to poetry,* and the poet returns to his poem: "Uh . . .

stupid song . . . that weather bonnet/ Is all gone now" (RAM, 53). The poet reiterates his program of unprogrammatic despair: "Remember,/ No hope is to be authorized except in exceptional cases/ To be decided on by me" (RAM, 53). A return to rule by grace and interior validation or verification is authorized. And the poet returns to his role as Freudian daydreamer: "In the meantime, back to/ dreaming,/ Your most important activity" (RAM, 53).

Desire for more normative relations disturbs the daydreamer, but his motto is also authorized in solipsistic categories: "Free but Alone" (RAM, 54). Like Magritte's lovers, with cloths over their heads and kissing blindly, Ashbery demands: "If you dream at all, place a cloth over/ your face:/ Its expression of satisfied desire might be too much for some/ spectators" (RAM, 54). The next paragraph is a strophe of ecstasy that is the quintessence of satisfied desires; it is not exactly a dream like the Voyage of Part II but it is an earthly paradise of memory, set like one last jewel manneristically in the center of Part III of "The Skaters." It begins with the recurrent "The west wind grazes my cheek, the droplets come pattering down" employed as lines one and three, interrupted by the Keatsian but more wisely passive question: "What matter now whether I wake or sleep?" (RAM, 54). In this passage of "sexual imagery" the poet attains another melodic height; the paragraph is seamless, but it also *parodies* Roethke's poems of childhood pleasures (among rural phenomena) and contains farm imagery reminiscent of the sunnily stippled poem of *The Double Dream of Spring:* "The Chateau Hardware" (p. 73).

This sexual paragraph is like the earlier "Voyage," not to be modulated "out of" but disrupted by a sudden image of misery: "The gray wastes of water surround/ My puny little shoal" (RAM, 54). Storms once again threaten an *already* shipwrecked poet. Fish lie rotting, perhaps seals, or, most likely, walrus, "odd-tusked monsters," in the sun, and are not even food for eating. The poet, Robinson Crusoe, now, deracinated, is necessarily climbing the rocks to scan distances for hopeful signs, not for a ship "of course" but at least for dolphins or whales. The birds are threatening him comically, and again the storm resumes: "The grass is low" (RAM, 55). The reader now realizes, of course, that like the fire-fountain, this Crusoe as an exotic image is at some time going to be punctured, but the poet keeps elaborating his "distances."

The poet, aesthetically, is trapped in his admiration for the storm and his need to be a pragmatic Crusoe: "I really had better be getting back down, I suppose" (RAM, 56). He lingers in the storm as he has previously lingered in other "puzzle pictures" and anxious dreams. "What difference does it make?" (RAM, 56). A certain torpor permits him to indulge this storm as aesthetic spectacle. "Supposing I catch cold? It hardly matters, there are no nurses . . ./ To make an ass of one" (RAM, 56). The poet indulges himself in a little case of "suicidal affect" and romantically catches cold: "Kerchoo! There, now I'm being punished for saying so" (RAM, 56). He apostrophizes both the Storm-fiend and the vultures of the island affectionately, in a comic passage reminiscent of the earthly paradises and sudden hells of Ashbery's contemporary, Kenneth Koch, who is an influence here.[8]

Suddenly the vision of "Crusoe as poet" dissolves to Ashbery's middle-class predicament. The poet has been apart from normative life, and the world of the newspaper, with its sudden changes and sombre destructiveness of the old orders: "A revolution in Argentina!" (RAM, 57). Ashbery's parody of Mayakovsky is short but an intense rupturing of prorevolutionary bliss or ardor: "Think of it! Bullets flying through the air, men on the move;/ Great passions inciting to massive expenditures of energy" (RAM, 57). A dismal apolitical indifference to this indifferent novelty is offered: "Here, have another: crime or revolution? Take your pick" (RAM, 57). Just as the newspaper's montage is discontinuous and unreal, so the poet leads us into a theme of his indifference and uncanny isolation and ostracism from it all: "professional exiles" (RAM, 57). *Agape* is disrupted, and even passing the sugar becomes an example of malice and dishonesty, of nonsense in the phrase: "Pardon me . . . a lot of bunk" (RAM, 57). Comraderie is impossible, *eros* disrupted, and the "motley spectacle" offers a charm only for a very peculiar genre of aesthetic pleasure: "Its defectuous movement" (RAM, 57). The Heraclitean flux is explicitly alluded to: "We step out into the street, not realizing that the street is different" (RAM, 57).

The poet of absence is ironically "filling a place" in friends' lives, just as the snowflakes are also ironically "stuck": "A few snowflakes are floating in the airshaft" (RAM, 58). The sun is descending and the shadows are equally tepid and gray. This luke-warm state, which Ashbery counterpoises to a real "change" and "passion" is suddenly parodied by uniquely isolated bits of dialogue from a golfing manual. Like alchemical formulae, these are the pietistic certainties by which the American forgets discontinuities and probabilities, only in the ludicrous machinery of arbitrary rules and enjoyments. "Any more golfing hints, Charlie?" (RAM, 58). The manual gives hints, unlike the poet, who is more wary with the explanatory power of discursive coherence. And the hilarity of this spectacle is summed up in the explosive parody: "All up and down de whole creation" (RAM, 58). The omniscient poet, like the Negro spiritual's God from *Job*, keeps pressing his wide-scale sweep in a bitter montage of stupidity and vertigo.

Ashbery, who has permitted himself the languors and loves of aesthetic illusion, here punctures the vapidities of the urban escapist. The poet may give up, throw "the whole business into the flames," because his real longing is not to "trick and manage" the irate reader, but "to be out of these dusty cells once and for all" (RAM, 59). He acknowledges the desire of a "real" salvation, but immediately, ironically, rejects the possibility of its immanence. The eschatological view is not seductive for the *persona*. "*His* day is breaking over the eastern mountains, at least that's the way he tells it" (RAM, 59). The authority of revelation is counterpoised with the theme of inner verifiability. The poet even sneers at his own automatic sneer: "You who automatically sneer at everything that comes along, except your own work, of course" (RAM, 59) and feels a merging and a Wordsworthian passivity: "To wake suddenly on a hillside/ With a valley far below—the clouds" (RAM, 59). The desire, however, for this dissolution and merging is also a "punishment."

The third part of "The Skaters" ends in a despairing vision of the poet, "like a plank/ Like a small boat blown away from the wind" (RAM, 60). Not blown away "by the wind" but "from the wind," the poet has been trapped in a calm, and he is without rudder and external motivation. Though it has its comic end ("It all ends in a smile somewhere" [RAM, 60]) and may have a literary future ("Notes to be taken on all of this" [RAM, 60]) and though the poet can see it, it is still pictured as "in the darkness" of his dreamy continuation of discontinuity. He lists the months of his "penance" in a drab catalogue: "January, March, February" (RAM, 59) of discontinuity and backward leaps and disjunction. "January, March, February" looks forward to the incoherent, solipsistic end in which the stars appear "in perfect order" (RAM, 63) though the order is not that of external reality, anywhere, but of a pleasurable dream in the labyrinth of the poet. "January, March, February" might be the motto of this poem, with its dips into lost childhood and lost dreams, "lost words" ("The Picture of Little J.A. in a Prospect of Flowers" [ST, 27]) and it certainly indicates that discontinuity and distorted chronology by which the poem operates. The postman, comically attacked by the hellish bulldog, is brought back, like a lost month or lost word or lost letter, in a sudden image, only to be punctured: "The true meaning of some of his letters is slight" (RAM, 59). I. A. Richards and C. K. Ogden have resumed the "meanings" of meaning.[9] Here Ashbery gives special poignancy to the meanings of meaninglessness, the meaning of slight meaning, of language at the *end*, the "banality which in the last analysis is our/ Most precious possession" (DDS, 39). The degraded is seen lucidly as degraded, but now freshly as the precious portent of our fallen and fractured world, where we are broken apart and yet whole like the landscapes of Cézanne. In the fourth part, the poet recapitulates and gives an enduring coda to this "shattering" theme.

The rhythmic mastery of Ashbery can be seen throughout this poem, but never more conclusively than in the intensity of the short Part IV, in which as Kenneth Koch has said, "it [the poetry] gives pleasure with almost every word" (RAM, jacket). A brilliant example is his recapitulation of the rhythm of the ecstatic "The west wind blows" passage from Part III, now turned into a dissonant: "The wind thrashes the maple seed-pods,/ The whole brilliant mass comes spattering down" (RAM, 60). "Mass" also reminds us of "the whole mismanaged mess" of the world of nineteenth-century causality, now spilled and smeared on discontinuous streets. The couplet is followed by a little parody of a Chinese "wan ending of defeat and humiliation." The poet, governor of *C* province (a curiously anonymous and nonexotic place), perhaps a professional exile himself, "a lad when I first came here," describes himself in terms reminiscent of the depositions of the first part: "old and uninteresting." The governor is "old but scarcely any wiser" (RAM, 60).

Wittgenstein's "ladder of propositions,"[10] which the Viennese logician said should be thrown away when one has reached the understanding that they are meaningless, has been called a paradox because, if the propositions are indeed meaningless, then it seems to be a ladder without rungs. Ashbery uses this bitter metaphor of climbing: "To slowly raise oneself/ Hand over hand, lifting one's entire weight" (RAM, 60) in a suddenly staggered and slow rhythm of short tetrameter: "That has always been behind you" (RAM, 60). "Freedom, courage/ And pleasant company" are possibilities that the poet is said to have forgotten. His movements have become comical and undignified, like those of Beckett's clowns. The whole fourth part of "The Skaters" is a last parade of clowns and failures, a parade of parodies. Even the last line, concerning the heavenly bodies, may be said to be "the biggest joke of them all." Even the spring is punctured and eucalyptus branches are called "baggy" (RAM, 60).

Once again in "The Skaters" an *exemplum* or paradigm is offered and reticently commented on: "The day was gloves.// How far from the usual statement" (RAM, 60). To emphasize the meaninglessness of it all, the poet gives, paradoxically, the simple statement, or gambit: "I mean this." This short infusion of colloquial certainty is the most unsettling fragment of all, comparable to a reminder in "The Hollow Men" of the Lord's Prayer, with its archaic certainty thrilling the reader with an arcane despair. "The day was gloves" is a statement that contains all the polysemy of a civilization of reification and discontent. In such obsessed condensations, our poet reveals mastery in defeat.

At this point in Part IV desperation and lyric intensity ensue: "The sands are frantic/ In the hourglass" (RAM, 61). This poem is, like O'Hara's "Meditations in an Emergency," not so much a meditation *on* an emergency, though that was O'Hara's original title (see *Collected Poems*, p. 532n), as a meditation inside and during an emergency. Even a static de Chirico-like image of a train sitting in a station becomes foreboding: the poet has dreamed that it might be moving. But the idea of a voyage has ended. The off-rhyme "motion and station" sadly and dissonantly emphasize the subtle distraction and dissatisfaction in this despair and waking torpor.

Parody of Kafka is then inserted: "a few travelers on Z high road./ Behind a shutter, two black eyes are watching them./ They belong to the wife of P, the high-school principal" (RAM, 61). A Chekovian fragment also, it reminds one that people have dwindled to literary symbols and disappointed metonymies, parts that cannot be taken for wholes. Literary allusion in "The Waste Land" usually referred to "high tradition." Here one does not know with any precision the source of the fragment, or what tradition it refers to, if any. As in "Europe," the *collagiste* fragment is offered for its own sake, a part of the discontinuity and cold externality of the poem.

In Chekov's theatre, a screeching door may conjure up a world of distraction. Here, too, the image is of a contingency and badly operating boundaries: "The screen door bangs in the wind" (RAM, 61). Not a storm, but merely an annoying detail, like that said by George Orwell to have humanized for him a man on his way to the gallows—a doomed man who avoided a puddle. Ashbery presents vividly these small, human and chance-ridden details, details in a world of dissolving masses. "I have all I can do to keep body and soul together" (RAM, 61). The simplest cliché, the precious banality, is raised by gallows humor to be an insight into our precarious balance: "And soon, even that relatively simple task may prove to be beyond my powers" (RAM, 61). There is a resumption too of the theme of meaningful if empty *silence:* "That was a good joke you played on the other guests./ A joke of silence" (RAM, 61). Here it is a deeply humiliating "joke." The aesthetic methodology has dwindled to mere malice, to domesticated squabbles in Chekovian misery which the poet knows is now a feeble reflection of the motives for a negative way: "That was a good joke" is also a way of deposing the joke. Rimbaldien silence, ruptures of normative life, will not work. A greater dissociation looms over "The Skaters" than can be remedied by a mere revolt or *enfant terrible* stance of shocking the middle class by silence.

Again, the image of spring is seized upon as a possible salvation through naturalistic union. "The spring, though mild, is incredibly wet" (RAM, 61). The poet has been blowing soap-bubbles, or remembering the ones of Part I (RAM, 40), and he senses his isolation with toleration and delight. Again, the rhythm reminds us of his distance, however, from childhood joys: "The birch-pods come clattering down on the weed-grown/ marble pavement./ And a curl of smoke stands above the triangular wooden roof" (RAM, 61–62). The poet's rhythm is at the furthest remove from the lyricism of the early melody: "The west wind grazes my cheek" (RAM, 54). Details are given with Robbe-Grillet-like geometrical flatness. Ashbery engineers his desperate distantiation.

Throughout the poem, Ashbery meditates upon the possible consolations of his aesthetic methodology. In Part IV of "The Skaters" the conclusion is given only after an exhaustive series of parodies of inconsolable mandarins and clowns of classic Chinese poetry: "Seventeen years in the capital of Foo-Yung province!" (RAM, 62). Woman as literary ideal is deposed, and sexual inversion is not offered as a glamorous possibility, though any nuptial possibilities are parodied and collapse. The wind stops, but the evening is insidious: "The evening air is pestiferous with midges" (RAM, 62). A puzzle-scene is explicitly offered: "There is only one way of completing the puzzle" (RAM, 62). The voyage has now begun, it is the voyage of the poet's new "loved one" who only appears in the poem to announce abandonment of the poet. "Announce your intention of leaving

me alone in this cistern-like house" (RAM, 62). Another empty
well is seen as the poet's home. The poet refuses to believe,
however, this abandonment, though it is announced *"meaning-
fully"* and accurately. Another parody of defeat is offered, this
time, of failure in jobs, in classic Chinese tones, as rendered
perhaps most painfully by the great Tang poet, Tu Fu, whose
most famous poem describes in detail the destruction of his frail
house in a storm. Here Ashbery's "house" is falling, and he
himself is collapsing in his own estimation: "The tiresome old
man is telling us his life story" (RAM, 63). This sentence of the
self in desiccation is well within the manneristic device of play-
within-a-play followed by sudden *repoussoir,* but now "The
Skaters" as a whole becomes the framed play and we realize
that the "life story" represents the entire poem. "Watching the
meaningless gyrations of flies above a sill" (RAM, 63, italics
mine) is yet another Chekovian fragment of despair. The flies
remind us of Shakespeare's "as flies to wanton boys/ so are we to
the gods." And also the gyrations of Blake's "The Fly." The poet
watches the discontinuous leaps of the fly as he has watched his
own timorous gyrations. Not the noble "gyres" of Yeats or Vi-
conian circles of Joyce, but the "meaningless gyrations . . .
above a sill." The gods have gone for good; only the words
remain.

The conclusion of "The Skaters" follows only upon the humble Chekovian: "The pump is busted. I shall have to get it
fixed" (RAM, 63). Not a Faustian remark, but a declaration that
life will be lived, not in daydreams, but a simple state of repara-
tion and work. Even *agape* or *eros* is resumed: "Your knotted
hair/ Around your shoulders/ A shawl the color of the spectrum//
Like that marvelous thing you haven't learned yet" (RAM, 63).
Breton's marvelous is possible, still. Ashbery insists on tiny curi-
osity and the desire to construct an intimacy, a poem.

Though the highest is postponed, the Fall is not insidious

JOSEPH CORNELL. Hôtel du Nord

3. Joseph Cornell. "Hôtel du Nord" (c.1953). Construction: glass, paper, and wood, 19 x 13¼ x 5½ inches. Collection of Whitney Museum of American Art. (Photo: Geoffrey Clements)

and is endured as both an aesthetic and ethical consolation: "The apples are all getting tinted/ In the cool light of autumn.// The constellations are rising/ In perfect order: Taurus, Leo, Gemini" (RAM, 63). The perfect order is a final irony, for there is no obvious season and no *locus* but the imagination in which the stars might rise this way. But this is a consolation: the poet's art can at last deceive us into believing a naturalistic illusion. If the medieval mind saw in the sky a reflection, an allegory of order, in our modern world one never seizes an allegory of anything but uncertainty, and that is no simple allegory. One must not humanize "everything"; the world is indifferent, if colorful. Consolation is given by the poem itself, in which the poet can create his own Joseph Cornell-like box with Renaissance perspectives leading to false conclusions. Ashbery rejects pieties and ends with a paradoxical conclusion: the stars rising in a perfectly arbitrary *order*. The antinomian rejects the old laws, the old order of Kantian "starry heavens above, moral order within," and seeks within an aesthetic order to elaborate his "exquisite theme." All externals are deleted but the language arranges another world.

Thus, Ashbery concludes his most thrilling monument of neoclassic wit. While he matures, in *The Double Dream of Spring* volume, to a quiet Wordsworthian ruralism, with superb evocations in an ever more humble and wise manner, the poetry of "The Skaters" is certainly never "improved upon." Here, the parodistic tone is always sparkling; the modulations from tone to tone always surprising yet inevitable; and the final qualified affirmation extraordinarily convincing. While "The Skaters" is a gigantic poem, the parts fit together and fittingly conclude in the stars. Not until "The New Spirit" and "The System" is Ashbery able to find a new manner that might as convincingly sustain a long poem. That new manner is one prosier, still parodistic in its clichés of devotion, and yet the new prose lacks, of course, the metrical tensions felt throughout "The Skaters," as in the Roethke parody. While Ashbery proceeds to an ever flatter and more exhaustingly dry wit in prose poems of scale, one must appreciate this "middle" maturity of metrical poise and tact. It is a fundamental accomplishment. A poem of isolation that exhibits the suffering from the release from Logos has produced a certain catharsis. Without bombast, with a constant defamiliarization of language and imagery, the poet has constructed an architecture of absence and desire.

CHAPTER 6

Meditations on Probability: Three Poems

John Ashbery's work triumphs in the three prose pieces in his late book, ironically entitled *Three Poems* (New York: Viking Press, 1972). Ashbery's effort has been consistently to break down, or *break through,* in the fashionable *avant-gardiste* phrase, genres and genre criticism. "The System," which is perhaps the densest of all Ashbery's works, was first published in the *Paris Review* (Paris, 1971), and, with the blessing of the author, under the heading of "prose." The three "poems," "The New Spirit," "The System," and "The Recital," are indeed within the "tradition" of convoluted confessions, couched in a poetic prose, such as Rilke's *The Notebooks of Malte Laurids Brigge.* These works are finally to be seen as three *antinomian* confessions, that is, finally confessions of discontinuity and revolt, but within the Christian tradition of antinomian or anti-legalistic heresies. Within the pieces, Ashbery enunciates a view that comes close to existentialist senses of ambiguity: reality is as discontinuous as risk. He couches his principle of principlelessness within a nostalgia for principles unique to his late work. This nostalgia for principles is almost, but not quite, a conversion, since the poet remains aesthetically and ethically

locked within the self-created labyrinth. Poetry's chief reference
is to its nonreferential status.

But the three poems also function as a tripartite narrative.
"The New Spirit" starts out as an analysis of a love affair and its
collapse. Gradually the "you" of "The New Spirit" takes on
more and more solipsistic dimensions. It is as if a real and elementary "other" comes and goes in this "you," who is at times
also the projection of the narrator. In "The System" only faint
relics and replicas of that "other" survive. In "The Recital" we
are left with a narrator talking about and to himself—though it
is a self that is also intermittently entangled in a "real" world.
Throughout these three poems, with their differentiations, Ashbery is involved in a mature scheme of somehow evolving form
out of fertile formlessness.

If my text seems metaphrastic in its procedures, I would
defend it a bit by appeal to Benjamin's sense of the commen-
tary. The poem deserves the kind of attention formerly paid to
the sacred text. Such linearity is always already interlinearity
and a montage.

"The New Spirit" is a work largely in prose, but this declaration is already difficult, for Ashbery's work has tended to make
these genre statements deliquesce. Generally, we have two atti-
tudes toward the terms prose and poetry in twentieth-century
criticism: The first regards the division as self-evident, as in the
remark, "The difference between prose and poetry is like the
difference between masculine and feminine. If you don't know
the difference, you're in trouble." Or, second, the attitude of
those who have been able to accept portions of, say, Joyce's
Ulysses, as *prose poetry*, because of rhythmic regularity, opposed to one's sense of "plain prose" as multitudinous and
nonrecurrent in its rhythms. Ashbery's poem "The New Spirit"
is particularly hard even on this looser definition, since the
prose here is rather irregular in the rhythmical sense, except for

brief passages. But this very looseness has been a trait of Ashbery's lyrics, also, and is part of his imitation of what he calls "the touching qualities of newspaperese."[1] In other words, where Rimbaud's *Illuminations* solve the problem of the prose poem by intensity of detail, a certain volupté of phrasing, Ashbery's prose tends to be largely in a drab style, the metaphors are usually homely, and long passages appear to be close to collages of homogeneous clichés. The works have been jocularly differentiated in interview by Mr. Ashbery: "One was prose and some poetry; the other did away with the poetry and didn't use indentations at all, the last was written in 'regular' paragraph form."[2] This blank, Warholesque statement should not lead one to degrade the "genre" problems posed by the three poems. Ashbery's is a furious critique of the usual bathetic imitations of voluptuous symbolist prose poems.

"The New Spirit" begins with an evocation of two aesthetic processes. The first seems to be the Whitmanesque inclusion of everything, the style of the *catalogue raisoneé;* the second, said to be "another, and truer way" (TP, 3) is the way of omission. This reminds us of the thematic of "leaving-out" as discussed in "The Skaters" (RAM, 39). However, the reader is immediately aware in "The New Spirit" of an unexpected flaccidity, a charming drabness to the opening, which is the extraordinary inversion of the rigorous and decorous introduction of "The Skaters." In both poems, however, the poet again reverts to the gambit of the poem discussing itself, in Wallace Stevens' manner. The irony of the beginning, however, seems to be that while the theory of aesthetic omission is expounded, the poem itself proceeds to a voluminousness, or rather rotundity, that has little to do with the lyrics of bare discontinuities to which this opening statement may be taken as referring. Ashbery is deleting deletion.

Examples of the aesthetic of discontinuity, lawlessness, antinomianism, or whatever one may prefer to call it, are then adduced: "clean-washed sea/ The flowers were" (TP, 3). These examples come suddenly; they are presented as little "collaged" bits, much as in Ezra Pound's device of a sudden fragment of an aesthetic past, which is however in this case the artist's own. The next statement clarifies: "These are examples of leaving out." But the artist immediately raises the problem of this aesthetic—it seems impossible not to have any example replaced, as with an abhorrence of aesthetic vacuum: "But, forget as we will, something soon comes to stand in their place" (TP, 3).

Ashbery is being perhaps purposely "dark" here, in the sense of using a language of the teacher who has pursued a path further than the student, and is pointing rather than showing, for his gnomic generality is followed again, purposely and crudely, by a connotatively encrusted vocabulary, exactly the vocabulary the Poet has hitherto so avoided except to parody. But here it is very difficult to identify the parodistic target: "Not the truth, perhaps, but—yourself" (TP, 3). It seems that the confession is now alluding to the personal stamp, the individualism, which *brands* the poetic object, and thus tends to take up the vacuum of the choice of choicelessness, or "leaving-out." This is Ashbery's allusion to Marcel Duchamp, whose very signature tended to *take up* the place of any other choice once he had gone beyond the "way" of "putting it all down" and on towards the selection of *objet trouvé*. Ashbery is discussing here the plight of *homo faber* and *homo laborans* in an aesthetic of "leaving-out," thus nondoing: his *playful* principle, "It doesn't matter whether it was difficult to discover America; it matters whether you discover it." A great deal of Ashbery's work, like some of Duchamp's and Warhol's work, is thus twisted on the *dadaist* principle of attempting to determine exactly how far a Wordsworthian "wise passivity" can be taken. We have seen Ashbery's passivity as regards *associationalism:* "As for free association, what else is there?"³ The reliance on Freudian free association then tends to lead to an automatism which becomes, despite itself, solipsistic, and so individuated as to evade stubborn externalities: "But the truth has passed on/ to divide all" (TP, 3). Ashbery, in the American pragmatic tradition, tends to reject here the extreme of automatism, through self-consciousness and parody. No association is free for the rigorous poem.

The problems of automatism—with its confusion of conscious and unconscious, and with comically direct allusion to Keats' famous questions—are posed immediately: "Have I awakened? Or is this sleep again?" (TP, 4). This question is immediately modulated in an extreme form of conscious parody of "religious confessionalism": "Another form of sleep? . . . The middle of the journey, before the sands are reversed: a place of ideal quiet" (TP, 4). Thus, the thematic of Dante's "middle of life's way" is revived, and with the Dantesque title of "The New Spirit," the reader is made aware that the work is intending at least a species of summation, of attempt at conversion, "awakening," that is. We are dealing here with what Rexroth once identified as Ashbery's "wisdom" in the Chinese manner, in the *Rivers and Mountains* volume, now translated into more specifically western vocabulary.⁴ Like the *Vita Nuova*, "The New Spirit" is a spiritual diary and stylistic critique.

The apostrophes in the following paragraph may seem to be the weakest part of the introduction of "The New Spirit." "You are my calm world. This is my happiness. To stand, to go forward into it" (TP, 4). The only relief from the slightly saccharine quality here is the immediately self-abasing sentences: "The cost is enormous. Too much for one life" (TP, 4). One might identify here a difficulty of the antinomian, the discontinuous: the difficulty of presenting a Buberian *Thou* in any three-dimensionality. Ashbery's attack on this position might be that a three-dimensional *Thou* is never intended, that the naturalist strain is at the furthest remove from this form of parodied "confession." One cannot however miss the feeling-tones of nostalgia for this three-dimensionality, and a seeming admission that the "sleep" of associationalism, and dream-logic, has led to the impasse in which the apostrophe to the beloved seems so weakened and brief. The poet will finally have an I-Thou relation with his text. For some, this is a horrible desiccation; for others, aesthetic honesty.

Imagery of absence, as seen in canonic remembrances of things past, then follow upon this paragraph of direct apostrophe. In Ashbery, as in the early "Picture of Little J.A. in a Prospect of Flowers" (ST, 27), the photograph is a sublimely simple image of man's passive resistance to mechanical reproduction. The photograph is the static event, easily montaged, ephemeral, liable to passive perversions of collection (as in the slingshot collector of "The Skaters" [RAM, 34]) and, with its *petit bourgeois* connotations, a visual-technical analogue of French potted flowers on windowsills: the repetitive, banal, manufactured image, seemingly inimical to the humane. In "The New Spirit," the photograph functions, like Eliot's famous catalogue of refuse at the beginning of "The Fire Sermon," as a *memento mori*, both a vestige and a Proustian *madeleine*. Here, as in the Church's use of recollection, there is a sign of Christian remorse: "Turning on yourself as a leaf, you miss the third and last chance" (TP, 4). There is only a slightly veiled autobiographical tone here; the narrative in "The New Spirit" is entangled, but never entirely hidden. A slight disjunction functions to produce "funny unexpectedness," but here it functions to lead expectedly toward the perdition of meaninglessness that is Ashbery's constant thematic: "to escape the ball/// of contradictions, that is heavier than gravity bringing all down to the level. And nothing be undone" (TP, 4). The phrase "to the level" is a witty evocation of the personal sinful despair, "depression," in which the *persona* finds himself, and out of which meaninglessness "The New Spirit" attempts to find *logos* but finds the plurality of words instead.

Much of the poem "The New Spirit" is an attempt to escape from the "level" and all "gravity." However, the usual Ashberyan devices of inscape, funny exoticism, or eroticism, do not seem to operate here. The most explicit rejection of escapism, seen as a flight from the anxiety of facing absurdity, is enunciated, and with mere traces of Ashbery's parodistic tones, which are of course never entirely absent: "We have broken through into the meaning of the tomb" (TP, 5). The problem with the sentence (as with the savage paradox of "The Skaters": "Only one thing exists: the fear of death" [RAM, 52]) is that *the tomb* is not *broken through*, that is, there is no traditional imagery of resurrection. What is broken into, and what entraps the *persona* of "The New Spirit," is the gravity of mortality, which is now being faced directly. The desire for the early earthly paradise, so intense elsewhere in Ashbery's work, is now merely wistfully posed: "And what about what was there before?" (TP, 5). Culminating poems in Ashbery, as in Eliot, tend to be at the extreme occasion of facing the misery of meaninglessness. Shorter lyrics, like Ashbery's "The Chateau Hardware," are often fine evocations of suburban pleasures—childhood musically appropriated for the present. The long poems tend to confront mortality without the jewelry and cornucopias. The scale itself matches the magnitude of the theme.

The question posed about the past is now answered, if obliquely: "This is shaped in the new merging" (TP, 5). It is difficult at this point to know what the poet means by his use of the plain, declarative mode. Is this really an answer to the question posed at the end of the previous paragraph, or are we led *post hoc propter hoc*, and faced with a misleading *non sequitur?*

The coherence of the following passage seems fairly assured, if darkened. The poet refers to novelty, but paradoxically likens it to "ancestral smiles, common memories" (TP, 5). In this sense the new merging is a merging with the traditional forms. But there is also a strangely juxtaposed, blasphemous, almost de Sade-like image of "the new merging": "To end up with, inside each other, moving upward like penance" (TP, 5). Imagery confusing sexual union and religious union seems here to be employed misleadingly: "For the continual pilgrimage has not stopped" (TP, 5). This yields a species of parenthetical hedonism, which involves a descent into childhood eroticism. But the whole poem is a lament of mutilated erotics.

The poet once again surrenders to what is mechanical in evolution: "There is nothing to be done, you must grow up" (TP, 6). The discussion of this surrender to growth is now accompanied by less operatic *sententia* on old age. "The pace is softening now, we can see why it had to be. Our older relatives told of this" (TP, 6). Still, the parodistic use of the encompassing "our" is peculiarly pointed and enlivening. In this lament, any evocation of adolescence is followed by a pathetic question concerning memory: "but will the memory call itself to the point of being? . . . it slips away, like the face on a deflated balloon, shifted into wrinkles . . . ." (TP, 6).

The discussion of old age, with its description of the old balloon, is another example of Ashbery's self-immolating persona, like the dwarf in "How Much Longer will I be able to inhabit" or Dido in "Two Sonnets," specifically self-consuming. The self-consuming parodies of Ashbery have led him, in Dorian Gray manner, to envisage himself as one wrinkled balloon "permanent and matter-of-fact, though a perversion of itself" (TP, 6). The balloon is paradoxically a toy and yet, like Li Po's fabled throw-away poems, a paradigm of the anxious situation of the contemporary poet, conjured up by W. H. Auden in the introduction to *Some Trees.*

The discussion now has so directly entered misery and mortality that the poet seems extremely justified in bursting into "song," if slightly loosened metrically, roughly analogous to the song at the close of Rilke's *Malte Laurids Brigge.* In Ashbery's song, "Hollow Man" imagery is pressed: "words broken open and pressed to the mouth" (TP, 6). The imagery also proceeds immediately and justifiably to the theme of precision in language and thought: "the fuzzy first thought" (TP, 7). Ashbery seems here to be leading to the most inclusive way of engulfing the "debris of living," a transforming *poetical* stroke: "To deal with or be lost in/ In which the silent changes might occur" (TP, 7). This statement suggests that the poem witnesses the silent evolution of the *persona,* and that 19th-century "suspense," eschewed by Ashbery elsewhere, is operative here. The poet has posed the extremes: "to deal with or be lost in" (TP, 7).

The disappointments of the dream logic of associationalism are then discussed in prose: "it had not yet begun, except as a preparatory dream, . . . which dwindled into starshine like all the unwanted memories. There was no holding on to it" (TP, 7). Some of the worthwhile, the less transitory aspects of the dream are seen to be its *paradigmatic* qualities, didactic, bearing the texture of one's waking life also: "It taught us forms of this our present waking life, the manners of the unreachable" (TP, 7). In this sense, Ashbery, like André Breton, Pierre Reverdy, and St.-John Perse, has used the arbitrariness of the dream as a *preparation,* now for a greater, "realistic" enucleation and self-assessment. The Christian imagery is used in a bantering tone: "For we judge not, lest we be judged," but the inexorableness of "objecthood" and the "cold external factors" resume: "yet we are judged all the same, without noticing" (TP, 7). The poet urges on a new courage, less dream-obsessed: the courage that comes when we accept the fact if not the validity of those judgments others made about us and put on the form their judgment has invented for us. "And in this form we must prepare, now, to try to live" (TP, 8) (a clear echo of Valéry's "il faut tenter de vivre" from his "Le Cimetière Marin"). Both the *persona* of the poem and the poem itself, desperately though with an outwardly sluggish or dandified air, try here to enucleate the quotidian through a profanely religious conversion to it. Ashbery the dandy begins to make his criticism of dandyism. He stops loitering and begins to think that he has had some problems with preciosity.

The next paragraph of "The New Spirit" is a kind of "dark night." In his discussion of the moon and painting the poet is hoping for a possible continuity, a possible coherence in a world largely "unmanageable, so indigestible" (TP, 8). But all the coherence is darkened with an explicit statement on the classic Ashberyesque theme of *concealment:* "No, but there comes a time when what is to be revealed actually conceals itself in casting off the mask of its identity, when the identity itself is revealed as another mask, and a lesser one, antecedent to that we had come to know and accept" (TP, 8). Though the author cannot be satisfied with "mutually amused half-acceptance" (TP, 8), he finds it the only possible way of beginning in the daylight— as opposed to the moonlit—world. Language and self are both reticences, and you cannot peel such reticence to a core.

What follows is another variation on the theme of "choice," and again it is in the particular "key" of "wise passivity," this time the significant verb being "discarding." The variation is now extraordinarily close to a mere echo of "The Skaters' " disquisition on the "leaving-out business." Self-parody seems evident in the ruminating: "This is the point of the narrowing-down process" (TP, 9). Randomness is also seen as a corollary to the rejection of conscious choice: "the new kind of arbitrariness" (TP, 9). A Shakespearean evocation of mortality is given a colloquial twist in the phrase "saw-toothed anomalies of time" (TP, 9). The poet, in free verse now, once again moves toward an evocation of the "Thou" of the poem ("You were always a living/ But a secret person" [TP, 10]) and this purely *poetic* interpolation begins to be more and more suggestive of the Dantesque interpolations of love songs in the *Vita Nuova,* except that Ashbery's songs are extraordinarily muted, short as a Webern piece, dissonant as the music evoked in "The Skaters," and ending with the crucial suggestion of rejection, frustration, inappropriate relations, loss of dignity, and comic *sequelae:* "And so, even more, a sign of what happens today,/ The glad mess, the idea of striking out" (TP, 10). The transition is not hurried, and is made with the mysterious interrogative: "was it you?" (TP, 10). The poet questions "the continent of eros" in Durrellian fashion: "For we never knew, never knew what joined us together" (TP, 10). An image of misery and geometrical perversion, analogous to the wrinkled balloon, is seen in the inorganic realization "of Roman engineers, a stone T-square" (TP, 10). But the poet accepts only the capricious curves of the organic, the "glad mess."

The comedy of disappointed erotics, of mismanaged and capricious relations are the subject of the sequel. "I am slurped into it, falling on top of you and falling with you" (TP, 11). Notice here the beauty of the juxtaposition of the quotidian vocabulary, and the careful management, not at all "messy," of the prepositions and prepositional phrases. The "harping" on the word "fall" is particularly Empsonian in its witty evocation of Christian and post-Christian disintegrations. Much of the "bare" style here reminds one of Stein in her compositional austerities of few nouns: "At this point it is again time for forgetting" (TP, 11). One should mention Ashbery's praise for the little-known volume of Stein's *Stanzas in Meditation,* as much as his admiration for her prose.[5]

Perhaps the most interesting development in "The New Spirit" is again the Gertrude Stein-like simplicity in which the poet "ruminates." We are far from the intensity of F. R. Leavis's "line of wit" and criteria of immediate presentation and intensity, but we are given instead much of the novelistic fullness of the great confessions of Stein. "To escape in either direction is impossible outside the frost of a dream. . . . Therefore I hold you. But life holds us, and is unknowable" (TP, 11). This passage reminds us of Rilke's famous "Love Song"[6] in which the lovers are said to be held by a sacred instrumentalist. Much of Ashbery's "New Spirit" concerns the Rilkesque *active passivity* in which cognition is labyrinthine, endlessly defeated. And yet what is granted through surrender is analogous to Luther's ideal of the *numen tremendum.* Here, the sacred is sensed more in sexual reverie than in the experience of an undifferentiated continuum, but the aesthetic continuum of a sacred *logos* is certainly pointed towards. The poet is beginning, in style and theme, an attempt to rise into a possible positivity.

Again, "The New Spirit" breaks into a species of *repoussoir* in free verse. The "poem" *comments* on the unfolding tale: "The motion of the story is moving though not/ getting nearer" (TP, 12). The following paragraphs have some of the exoticism of "Villes" and "Ville" of Rimbaud: "All eyes are riveted to its slowly unfolding expansiveness" (TP, 12). The allusion to Frank O'Hara's epithet, "Grace to be born and live as variously as possible,"[7] is the only self-effacement, but a strong one: "Progress to be born" (TP, 12). This is a "shapeless modest tale" (TP, 12). The next paragraph reverts again to the idea of absence, a reminiscence of Rimbaud's abdication: "You know that emptiness that was the only way you could express a thing?" (TP, 12). The "Thou" of "The New Spirit" is seen, Beatrice-like, to wish the poet to be lifted from this emptiness, his predicament, but the paragraph is dramatically disjunct, and the phrase inserted by itself, far to the right of the margin, is the pathetic "reading without comprehension" (TP, 13). Again, frustration of meaningful coherence is seen as part of the discontinuity of realism: "Cold, piecemeal renderings"; and dislocation, fragmentation are explicitly rendered: "In you I fall apart" (TP, 13), a new variation on the theme of "falling," descent, and despair. The poet attempts an apostrophe in the most direct manner, again, as if his needs were becoming increasingly difficult to conceal, and *relation* itself more exacting: "To you:/// I could still put everything in and have it come out even" (TP, 13). But the poem's addressee is just a shifter, a relational zone, a zone of pathos and a warning sign.

The emptiness of aesthetic passivity is now compared with the plenitude of a "fully lived life." The "meaning of meaninglessness" theme is explicitly rendered in "Far from the famous task, close to the meaningless but real snippets that are today's doing" (TP, 14). The "task" is comparable to Christian vocation, but the environment is now poignantly bare and post-Christian. The task is to deal with the cold externalities growing within, and the cold discontinuities mechanically emplaced without. The poet of "The New Spirit" is aware now that a new kind of mastery is required, but is unnecessary, since he is already part of this "discontinuous continuum": "a way of intermittent life, and the point was that the moments of awareness have to be continuous if they are to exist at all. . . . To be living, in each other, the perfect life but without happiness" (TP, 14). The poet seems condemned to "commenting" on the flux of his spirit even in the act of not commenting, and the negation itself has become so customary that the artist is aware of the comical authority, and even dignity, now granted the act of negation. One senses that Ashbery is here renouncing the pomposities of con-

tinental existential dicta, those documents of the 20th century
so infamously poised above the abyss without losing any of their
rhetorical poise and position. The sadness of Ashbery's tone is
thinner, colder, than the rhetorical nauseas of Sartre or Simone
de Beauvoir, though close to the epithets and laconicism of
Cioran. The poet addresses himself, not as within a psychoanalytic session, or as a *philosophe*, but as a suffering unity. The
world is a vale of text-making as of soul-making; and both tasks
are difficult, congruent, possibly identical.

The psychic sense of unreality is again confirmed by the poet:
"like a river which is never really there because of moving on
someplace" (TP, 15). This is a variation on the familiar themes
of the river in flux: If one never crosses the river twice, says the
pupil of Heraclitus, perhaps one never crosses the same river
even once, and Ashbery picks up this late and dismal corollary
to question, in a muted, blunt and passive fashion, the direct
"there-ness" of reality. The idea of some cosmic "hoax" is
raised, a comical analogue to the sense of "hoax" in philistine
reaction to *avant-gardisme*.

The poem here reads like an essay on deracination and the
Need for Roots. It gives us some sense of the bitter implications
of flux in Ashbery: "Smoke" is seen as "purified," but also drifting passively and alive only in so far as paradoxically "having
lost life at last" (TP, 15). The poet could resort to a *catalogue
raisonné*, "my rarest thoughts and dreams," but rarity is *not* the
goal here. Once again, in its bitter entrance, what is acknowl-
edged is the burden of everyday meaninglessness, the over-
whelmingly businesslike nature of the dreadful loss and defeat
within discontinuity. The smaller poems of the poet, like the
songs of "The New Spirit," are now seen to be exactly inclusions
on the plane of mere thoughts and dreams. This is also a critique of the rarified diction of the early Wallace Stevens, and a
pointing towards this final meditational technique of the aus-

terely drab, relieved only in its parodies of other prose voices, Henry James, for example. The rich parodies serve, however, to reemphasize the drabness of meaninglessness and a dry earnest search for wholeness. Language in Ashbery is that chaotic wholeness.

Throughout the earlier parts of "The New Spirit," Ashbery attempts to lead his own *persona* and poetry out of incoherence and despair: "there always comes a time when the spectator needs reassurance" (TP, 16). Any representation seems humorously and paradoxically doomed by affectlessness, disproportion, or a too-rigid congruence which the poet disdains: "So that we must despair of all realism now, because it is there, it is totally adequate for what was being represented, only we cannot feel it as such, but that is our tough luck" (TP, 17). There is presented the germ of an incipient belief in values, and in a formerly castigated sense of cosmic value: "we have the success of our gradual, growing belief in the importance of the universe" (TP, 17). The poet begins to analyze the problem of masochism in his abrogations of coherence: "Is it then that/// we wanted the whole thing to misfire?" (TP, 17). One is reminded of Rimbaud's rejection of the literary world in his furious, resentful letters, and his gradual affirmations of scientistic progress and enlightenment earlier castigated in the more resentful passages of *Les Illuminations*.

But the poet is still without precepts and illuminating insight except that all or *any* insights will do: "everything is a way, none more suitable nor more accurate than the last, oblivion rapidly absorbing their outline like snow filling footprints" (TP, 17). There is ironical allusion to *Ecclesiastes:* "To every thing there is a season," with a bitter emphasis on the reifying sense of "every thing" (TP, 18). Imagery reminiscent of Jasper Johns' "pop" maps, are suggested as both insidious in their disproportions ("They can join, but never touch" [TP, 18]) and menac-

ingly vapid. Ashbery has indeed suggested that he finds his poetry analogous to Jasper Johns' "lazy exploration of the self."[8]

"What is wanted is some secret feeling of an administrator"
(TP, 18) and "The New Spirit" is both an admission of a nostalgia for pietism, deistic belief and conscience, and a rejection
of any mere nostalgia: "There must be nothing resembling nostalgia for a past which in any case never existed" (TP, 19). Li-
turgy is summoned only to be abused for its false sense of closure and didactic coherence: "So ends the first lesson: that the
concave being," etc. (TP, 20). Wise passivity is now explicitly
alluded to in the phrase "erect passivity," a slightly active variation on the Wordsworthian theme: "a sort of house-arrest of the
free agent intentionally cut off from the forces of renewal, ob-
liged to spend a certain penitential time of drawing in and not
utilizing those intuitions that gave wings . . ." (TP, 21). The
persona has taken a stance, but the stance is without mobility,
like Eliot's "gesture within motion."

The businesslike world is a sordid reminder of the civilization
which, as Ashbery finds it, cannot reassure the value of novelty
in poetry and life: "the group's reluctance to fully celebrate
anything new" (TP, 21). The *persona* must renovate himself, but
with a curious distance in tone: "As in a novel . . . your character comes crashing through, . . . meanwhile the tale itself . . .
got up and did a dance and left" (TP, 22). The poet, as in the
business world of philistinism, feels distant from his works and
their sequential meanings. The "Bundle of incidents" that
makes up the plot here is likened to the "fundamental absence"
of "The Skaters," which also sought to be hypostatized and
leave on its own comical volition. But the adventure has become encrusted with older despairs: "there is very little romanesque element, more the ugliness of waiting and the obscenities
we think and speak, this is more like it" (TP, 22). The poet gives
into "realism" only as into a humiliating associational stream.

His dignity is again, at best, immobile and peculiar as his prose. Mimesis and antimimesis do not argue. The poet will use anything in desperation or revolt. The poem is an emblem, almost a utopia of desire and absence. Like Maurice Scève, who inspired Ashbery's long "Fragment," such poetry dazzles us with its persistent negativities.

The finest image of self-laceration in Ashbery is given in "The New Spirit" in mythological and glamorous terms, somehow subtly corroded: "A chariot going down kicking and struggling at the first brush with the sun's deleterious rays" (TP, 25). Here Ashbery assumes the role of Phaeton, as if to remind us that a poet, too, is a reckless adventurer. Like Ashbery, the youth, no matter how mortal, dares to approach the Sun, and is led astray by the wild dislocation of his own wishes: to assume control of the grotesquely powerful sun-chariot. But Ashbery sees this as a "melodramatic ending" from which he saved his own adventurous introspections and dislocated narratives and wishful poems, by the sense that coherence itself was somehow "desired" by chaos: "It was waiting for us: the sense that we must now put our ideas together and use them as steps for attaining some kind of rational beauty" (TP, 26). "Growth without change" is offered now instead of juxtapositions and montage, an "English garden" instead of a collagiste "Europe." The poet speaks to his lover in his "pleasant desert" with its "warpless and woofless subtleties" (TP, 29). This is an explicit appraisal of the seamless pattern in Ashbery's carpet, and in this centreless world, where all has once fallen apart, and where any ceremonies of innocence have been drowned, Ashbery does not await a Yeatsian second coming. Like Beckett's characters, he simply waits. His uncertainty is that of a wanderer who risks much by his lack of orientation: "It is like approaching a river at night, uncertain of the direction of the current. But the pulsating of it leads to further certainties. . . . For the moment uncertainty is banished at the same time that growing is introduced almost surreptitiously" (TP, 31). Indeed, Ashbery provocatively replaces his older theme of insecurity with the theme of supported evolution. Growing, with the risks of growths, ends uncertainty with sudden, pulsating possibilities.

While growth has been a theme before in Ashbery's poetry, it is usually jerky growth of adolescent embarrassments, as in "Our Youth" and "How much longer": growth in a school, or a "prison disguised as a school," not of the poet's making, but foisted upon him as a cold external. Usually, growth has been seen as something as automatic as a nightmare, as the apple tree at the beginning of "The Recital," giving nameless terrors for the poet to name. But in "The New Spirit," happiness is figured as the corollary to the "erect passivity" by which the poet, in a newly contrived prose of affirmation, underlines his own continuous evolution. Thus the poet can comment on the manners of his literary past, and affirm, as at the end of "The Recital," the way by which *poetic adventure* creates its own reward, its own form out of fertile formlessness, and redeems the precarious incoherences it may represent.

Poesis and evolution, growth within poetry, is seen to be the only redemptive adventure, and one which makes any other adventure seem "melodramatic" or "romanesque." The sense of this subtle, redemptive growth within a "moral universe" is reinforced by a reference to the philosopher Kant: "the philosopher's daily walk that the neighbors set their watches by" (TP, 32). Though Ashbery ends with a starry heaven that lacks the profoundly Pietistic species of order that Kant reflected upon with zeal, still Ashbery has accepted in his later work the wisdom of the perhaps comical restraints in the acceptance of measure. An image of *sophrosyne,* or wholeness, is slightly, ironically represented in the funny, compulsive punctuality of the philosopher. Even the city, given this "new spirit," can be do-

mesticated in a songlike intrusion: "Yet it was almost enough to
be growing up in that city/ . . . That metropolis was like the
kitchen of the world" (TP, 33). The city is not depicted as collapsing but as serviceable, as the poet has grown up enough to
be "setting out on the task of life" (TP, 34), as on a tour of duty.

A canonic image of happiness for Ashbery's favorite poet,
Friedrich Hölderlin, was a family in which every member had
his musical place, and so Ashbery's usual world of lapsed *logos*
now changes in sudden resonant verse: "So this meaning came
to arise/ Towering above the rest/ With a place for each member
of the family/ And further up in the hierarchy/ For every
thought and feeling that had passed or would come to pass" (TP,
34). Rather than the fear of death being the only thing in existence, the world is now seen warmly to exist, since the idea of it
exists: "And so the meaning is brought down/ To be with us
together, never the same again" (TP, 34). This passage is the
moment of *conversion to coherence* in Ashbery's poetry, and it
is followed by a line which suggests D. H. Lawrence's apocalyp-
tic songs: "We have passed through" (TP, 34). And here the
poet is not merely referring to a growth in style, but to a growth
in what might be thought of as "the normative sense of life" in
its Tolstoyan wholeness. Here growth is the architecture of his
peaceful poem.

"The calm illumination" is said by the poet to persist, and one
of its first effects is to lead him away from the glamorous and insidiously enchanting world of daydreaming and the world of
mere association: his early surrealist modality of stylish dreams
without *logos*. "And suddenly you have been occupied for some
time with unlearning . . . You forget . . . those morning
dreams whose aim was both to mislead and instruct" (TP, 35).
But the problem, as with Tolstoy's Levin, is the sense of the
strange lack of an Other to share the conversion: "a stranger for
you in your own home" (TP, 36). But the conversion is renewed

by a "golden exuberance," in a quiet scene enacted in a train (TP, 37). Light is now seen as metaphysical and sacred, not the miniature searchlights of "Europe," but "tiny points of light like flares seen from a distance" (TP, 37). Growth is once again possible, though it is a mature growth without attention toward advancement or fruits: "action without development, a fixed flame" (TP, 37).

But suddenly Ashbery suggests that the memorable conversion is "dead for many years," and that the period of this incandescence has perhaps been an abnormality and with few of the long-lasting effects of a true conversion (TP, 38). The pitfall of this incandescence was its lack of what Eliot might call *tradition*. The poet's graceful, almost Hindu reliance on a nonsensuous perception of the undifferentiated flux was not sufficient. The fixed flame is disrupted and quickly modulated away from in the next poem or lament: "The change is not complete" (TP, 39). And yet the happiness is retrospectively resumed: "We were ideally happy" (TP, 41). At least in memory, the poet sees a "field of narrative possibilities" (TP, 41). Tender principles are for the first time given as distinct possibilities of *ethos* in the quotidian world: "You wish you could shake hands with your lovers and enemies" (TP, 42). Tarot imagery, used so insidiously by Eliot in "The Waste Land," is here employed as imagery of pseudo-Christian affirmation: "the Hanged Man points his toe at the stars, at ease at last" (TP, 42). The theme of growth is developed in the fine image of a wounded card, from whose blood leaves and flowers spring.

Astrological imagery in Eliot signifies superstition or gnostic heresy of Faustian self-referentiality. Ashbery also employs astrological terms, but to affirm at least some illumination from a principle not quotidian, degraded, "sordid or insignificant." The parodistic tone however is still employed, to mock or delight in fashionable horoscopes: "The Ram is imbued with tremendous force. . . . He wants to go it alone" (TP, 44). Meanwhile, the poet has taken on a grandiose responsibility, in a spring of youthful "buzzing" and "sexing": "he had taken the universal emotional crisis on his own shoulders" (TP, 45).

The possibility of a vatic role is merely comic. The poet lapses into a "reflective voluptuousness" which he has previously condemned; even the sensuality is now vanished, and the reflectiveness too may be seen as "thinking of nothing at all." When he searches he finds pure tautology: the "great Common Denominator" proving "$ax^2 = ay^2$" (TP, 47). Here Ashbery uses the congruence of x and y as a heartbreaking image of the opaque end of all the fields of possibilities and growth. Stasis has become a mathematical misery of the emotions. The poet, however, offers a few fragments of poems: "As though the spark might not be extinguished," and utters vatic thoughts to "you born today" though "there was no one within earshot" (TP, 48–49).

The audience of "The Recital" streams out of the hall; here, there is no audience, and the earlier possibility of love has evaporated. Ashbery at the poem's end advocates "immobility" and contempt for those who would "better themselves at the expense of humankind in general" (TP, 49). His third-person prophet counsels from his own experience of the miraculous the acceptance, in the Hindu sense, of work without attention to its fruits. He catalogues his previous modes: bestial infant, hedonistic aesthete, and magnanimous lover. He sees them as a Tower of Babel that he has constructed: labyrinths—poems—to be abandoned.

Still, imbued with "the new spirit," he concludes that growth points to the future: "A new journey would have to be undertaken" (TP, 51). The major question is still the wonder of being and this is "again affirmed in the stars" (TP, 51). The stars pose no question, but the poet must, comically or not, strive to begin to answer that form of the question, which their very existence *is*. The stars, as in "The Skaters," are an emblem of wonder, the poet's almost coherent wonder at incoherent being, a being which he must formulate in a new prose-poetry, because it is not merely a "rhetorical question" but a problem of life, of vital language.

"The System" is couched in the clichés of religious confessions, as is "The New Spirit," and like "The New Spirit" it bears partly the dramatic narrative of a near-conversion, with no interpolations, however, of songs and poems. The prose in "The New Spirit" seems more rhythmically intense than in "The System," where the admitted influence[9] of Giorgio de Chirico's novel *Hebdomeros* is felt most acutely in the long sentences with their interminable hyphenations and parentheses, leading only to *cul-de-sacs:*

> Yet so blind are we to the true nature of reality at any given moment that this chaos—bathed, it is true, in the iridescent hues of the rainbow and clothed in an endless confusion of fair and variegated forms which did their best to stifle any burgeoning notions of the formlessness of the whole, the muddle really as ugly as sin, which at every moment shone through the colored masses, bringing a telltale finger squarely down on the addition line, beneath which these self-important and self-convoluted shapes added disconcertingly up to zero—this chaos began to seem like the normal way of being, so that some time later even very sensitive and perceptive souls had been taken in: it was for them life's rolling river, with its calm eddies and shallows as well as its more swiftly moving parts and ahead of these the rapids, with an awful roar somewhere in the distance; and yet, or so it seemed to these more sensible than average folk, a certain amount of hardship has to be accepted if we want the river-journey to continue; life cannot be a series of totally pleasant events, and we must accept the bad if we also wish the good; indeed a certain amount of evil is necessary to set it in the proper relief: how could we know the good without some experience of its opposite? (TP, 59)

The argument is fairly simple, but the stylistic mannerism of length itself should be observed as Ashbery ritually extends and

It is, however, not at all an arbitrary, homogeneous streaming of clichés. It does present its analysis of the clichés of religious predicament, the impossibility of cognition, within a peculiarly disturbing syntactical *grotesquerie*. However, it does not necessarily convince one that flaccidity need be ridiculed so long in the interests of pragmatics and kinesis. It is true, of course, that its monotonous horrors and sinful despairs are "a kind of" Purgatory, one which "The Recital" ends with the consolation of a *poesis* at once refined and tight.

An analysis and paraphrasis (or *metaphrasis*, since the poetry of uncertainty leaves no analysis untroubled) of the 29 paragraphs of "The System" must be a proper procedure. Ashbery has described the poem as one of a "wry, quasidialectical language to tell a love story with cosmological overtones" (TP, blurb). Paraphrase has its obvious pitfalls of overemphasizing linearity to the detriment of the poem's overt "dialectics." Taking William Empson's analyses as paradigmatic I shall not eschew the mode of consecutive analysis, even though the problematic of the poem resists simple "unravelling."

In paragraph one (TP, 53), the first short sentence is followed by a funny, lugubrious one of the length admired by Ashbery in de Chirico's *Hebdomeros*. "At this time of life" the poet's being is involved in a passive "listening" to the being external to it, the "weather" which is both the weather of natural passions and a naturally indifferent weather (TP, 53). Playfulness is announced as part of the mastery of this reality. But paragraph three (TP, 54) describes a painful "hysterical staccato" that remains and cannot be mastered by any simple regression or surrealist infantilism.

Paragraph four (TP, 54) evokes a time before the collapse into apathy. Just as Pasternak punned on vitality by giving his Dr. Zhivago the name that translates as "Dr. Living," Ashbery refers specifically to the theme of vivacity: "It was all life, this truth, you forgot about it and it was there" (TP, 55). Pity and solicitude also seems to have existed: "inside . . . an alphabet, an alphabet of clemency" (TP, 55). This was a time before the dilemma of solipsism: "The feelings never wandered off into a private song" (TP, 55). The poet wants to present "inner space" paradoxically "in the round," like those painters and poets, Ponge and Jean Helion, whom Ashbery loves for their cult of the surface.

In paragraph five (TP, 56) the nostalgic evocation is of natural coupling, as in the passage in "The Skaters" concerning the "horse and mare [that] go screwing through the meadow" (RAM, 54). (This passage was evidently inspired by one of Schoenberg's *lieder*.[11]) "The heaven-sent partner" is delineated with purposely archaistic verbiage and clichés of sin, frivolity, and idleness (TP, 57). Love is seen both as scourge and exaltation. Like de Sade, Ashbery here takes pleasure in describing vice in sacred terms. This is also obviously a form of degradation of the exalted as seen in all his parody. Allegorical and outmoded devices are degraded: "plagued by thorns, chased by wild beasts" (TP, 58). Polyphony as a method is described, and the theme of discontinuity again treated: "gorgeous, motley organism" (TP, 58), but of all the banalities, religious banality in particular is parodied: "There is no cutting corners where the life of the soul is concerned" (TP, 58). However, the terrible pathos admitted by Ashbery is that the banalities are both degradations and positivities. They are not merely being presented and juxtaposed to be "freshened up" in a Mallarméan procedure of rendering the "dialect of the tribe more pure."

The sixth paragraph (TP, 59) *bathes* us again—with much water imagery in the verbs—in the fluidity of dreams. Chaos itself seems normative or quotidian. Archaic imagery is used again, and of these devices the "river journey," as in "The Skaters," is again employed but with a minimum of drama (TP, 59). The need for evil is also explored and the clichés of Manichean piety ridiculed. "All that was necessary were patience and humbleness" (TP, 60). The way of piety is mocked by a sense of potent directionlessness. The way of piety seems too designed for the artist of automatism and dreams. He assigns the overly designed to the business world; accident and personal touch to the artist and poet.

In the seventh paragraph (TP, 60) the imagery is purposely and parodistically torpid: "pendulum . . . magic hand" (TP, 60). The true Earthly Paradise is seen in all autistic, *avant-gardiste* freedom as a "haphazard field of potentiality," sought amid the menaces of the more constricted or manufactured pieties (TP, 60). The eighth paragraph (TP, 61), beginning "Who has seen the wind," takes its infantile question as a rehearsed and obvious evocation, yet the question too retains a feeling-tone of pathos. Every moment can be revolutionary in the antinomian programme, but the continual crisis of salvation "at hand" renders movement hysterical and undignified, as in a speeded-up film. "Eternal vigilance" might well be eternal *rigor mortis*, and the pious ones, "in sackcloth," who make not the least impression on external reality, give but the impression of choice. Yet they remind one of the idea of possibility (TP, 62).

In a parody of Lewis Carroll's paradoxically static and running Queen, Ashbery describes the world in which points or terminations are never reached: "an end to the 'end' theory" (TP, 64). The poet would like to stop somewhere for the night, but the reposeful *locus* cannot be managed. The usual Ashberyan device is to present the comical possibilities of a poet confused by his paradoxical advance and stasis. Thus, the tenth paragraph (TP, 65) begins with a journalistic resumé of the year occurring on "the last day of January" "on Sunday" with a species of New Year's resolutions and sermon offered. But the feeling-tone is one of disorientation in a new month. Time is presented as a horrifying compulsion. Others are placid and the poetic image is obscured in a night amid passivity: "no urge to get up and put on a light" (TP, 66). The balance-sheet of the New Year goes unwritten: "there is something to be said for these shiftless days, each distilling its drop of poison until the cup is full; there is something to be said for them because there is no escaping them" (TP, 67). The poet bows his head in a whimsically logical acquiescence to the ineluctable comedy of consecutiveness and temporality. One of Ashbery's great charms is his constant ability to manage a stoical humanism that never ceases to maintain opportunities for self-pity and ambivalence. It is a poor stoicism that does not remind us, somehow, of the unuttered or unutterable complaint.

In the eleventh paragraph (TP, 67) the concept of metonymy dominates. Love can be deduced from lust, just as a botanical description may give us a conception of a flower (TP, 67). Perhaps this form of parodistic cognition, theory and model, is the only available resource. Perhaps, also, this is how poetic details work (TP, 68). The "erratic approach" to life is praised, just as Quixote seems more valuable than the Sancho Panzas of mere sense. The Quixotic quest, with all its erratic approaches to imaginary windmills is, then, "surely the way," and again paradoxically the way is "no way" (TP, 69).

"The great careers are like that," announces paragraph twelve, but with a certain irony connoting that their less erratic approaches all end in annihilation. Love is theme: the combination of bodies that seem imperilled by the falling darkness. The poet is lost and wants to get "more lost (an impossibility, of course)" (TP, 70). Careers are analogues to narrative in fiction; they are degraded plots that have forgotten the possibilities of freedom in living and combining (loving) in a more antinomian and graced directionlessness.

Ashbery then develops and comically deflates the "life-as-ritual concept," giving only the funny definition that "according to this theory no looking back is possible" (TP, 70). The poem itself is grainily concerned with the possibilities of a recovery of lost time, and Ashbery links this recovery with ideas of artistic gratification. Varieties of happiness are explored, called "frontal" and "latent" (TP, 71). The first is experienced as an urgency when help is required and is defined as a species of joyful dependency. This continues with corollaries of happiness, and the poet imagines the illegible mosaics of heaven in churches that the tourist peers at and abandons, content that they are there. Ashbery's *persona* is often this wry, quasidialectical tourist, peering at meaningless mosaics which seem to limn some degraded celestial happiness. But in "The System" all real happiness is now earthly and probabilistic.

"Latent happiness" is described by the poet as comparable to periods before spring. Ashbery has described his interest in "the pleasant surprise,"[12] and the constant expectation, constantly humiliated or gratified partially, constitutes this almost substantial happiness. Perpetual anxiety is delineated and pietism mocked: "they believe that they are thinking of nothing but God" (TP, 74). Constant uncertainty, *a contradiction in terms*, reminds us that Werner Heisenberg's laws of uncertainty are indeed laws, and that for the anxious neurotic, nothing becomes so static as an endless and anxious "advance," as in the Carrollian and Zeno-esque "running Queen," later to be explicitly taken up. Zeno's paradox for Ashbery has this corollary: there is no final resting place. Are we even moving? Here the menacing question is forgotten by the sensuality of aesthetic particularization. Art rescues the artist from vertigo and paradox by forcing him to pay attention *en détail* and to outline these details in poetry. Art, as Ashbery delineates it here, is concern, solicitude for these details. Art is never *en bloc*.

But what is the value of the detail? Ashbery makes this theme a flamboyantly developed one. These details are like the crumbs distributed by the usual Ashbery dwarf, now pictured as "Hop-o'-My-Thumb" (TP, 81). The crumbs remind us, again, in a Wordsworthian vein, of the redemption of the humble in Ashbery. Minute particulars are our nourishment and our guides: "And so all these conflicting meaningless details" (TP, 82).

After this meditation on detail, Ashbery modulates towards a metaphysical image of light as both fixed and moving, like the famous dance in Eliot's "Burnt Norton." The redemption of the crushed dream of happiness is that it is a dark light that shines on greater glooms. This stoicism and irony is not merely a pose and a temptation. It has been offered by Ashbery as his tentative rejection of any Eliotic pessimism. In dreams and automatism, rejected by Eliot in the late Christian works, the poet of "The System" recovers. He understands the "private language" of objects talking to each other (TP, 84). Their *arcana*, rejected by Eliot as part of the baggage of superstition is a partially understandable and endearing *arcana*. Ashbery's lights are intransigently secular.

But despair at pointless infinity follows. "Even the sun seems dead" (TP, 84). The Zeno-esque paradox seems necessary and immortal as a dream: "When will you realize that your dreams have eternal life" (TP, 85). Dreams are described as endearing exteriorizations and praised for their automatic qualities, as opposed again to the streamlined rigidities of manufactured objects. Eliotic darkness is mere spleen, while the reality of dreams seems *a new arrangement, a new system* (TP, 85). Given this supportive illumination, the dwarf changes to Prince Charming, before whom all doors open (TP, 86). Now air and life are images of a speedy if purposeless gratification (TP, 87).

In paragraph sixteen (TP, 87), the *persona* of "The System" with recovered vitality and independence attempts a more prehensile poetics. Ideals themselves may be forgotten, specifically the ideal of Keatsian pleasure. The everyday must be returned to though the everyday is a labyrinth: "The dank barren morass (or so it seems at present)" (TP, 88). The secret order there is one of "secret growing" and a process of maturation is described. Companions and strangers are viewed with benevolence and friendship. An end is now possible, even "the end of the world in no unfavorable sense" (TP, 89). One sees this as a parody of the gloomy apocalyptics of Rimbaud's "As one walks, it is only toward the end of the world" (my trans., "Enfance," *Les Illuminations*). Apocalypse for the antinomian, Ashbery, is merely a pleasant surprise or an anticipated pleasant surprise.

In the eighteenth paragraph (TP, 90), or strophe in prose, clichés of the "road less taken" are exhumed. Carroll's Red Queen is explicitly taken up and her impractical schemes, like the poet's own, can neither be abolished nor abandoned. Drenched in this irrationality, the poet feels the past has now a "sweetness [which] burns like gall" (TP, 91). He is like an uncertain dog on a busy street and is looking for a bone (TP, 91). Even more pitifully, he is even uncertain "what to ask for" (TP, 91). The poet then apostrophizes his own soul, a poet-dog, like Kafka's Philosopher-Dog. The poet announced that his sad stare is not a result of self-pity but concentration. As the dog looks for crumbs, the poet looks for details, and like Childe Roland he realizes that victory is "only reasonably certain" (TP, 92). Spring falls like a *musique concrète:* "magnolia petals flatten and fall off one after the other onto the half-frozen mud" (TP, 93) in a detail reminiscent of the defeated thaw of the last part of "The Skaters."

The poet has been limning a "chronicle play of our lives" in a parodistic text "crammed with action," like Ariosto or the *Encyclopedia Brittanica* (TP, 93). Kenneth Koch (interview, 1972) has spoken too of the joys of simple narratives, the early Christian mystery plays, Peter Pan, cartoons, Italian Renaissance epics. And this action-crammed pageant is valued by Ashbery "though we cannot tell why: we know only that our sympathy has deepened" (TP, 94). Actor and audience "mingle joyously" in a breakdown of conventions comparable to the breakdown of inhibitions in much "naive" slangy wit. But eschatology is not the point, just the lucidity of this "next-to-last act" where meaning has been rescued from meaninglessness: the meaning of the *penultimate*, where man seems stranded forever if forever advancing, longing perhaps pietistically for the "Ultima ultima Thule" but more modest in his aesthetic appreciation of the haphazard field of probability.

In "The System" Ashbery senses the conceit of apostrophizing the whole universe. The beloved is looked at as a detail in the cosmic welter and a dialogue is initiated (TP, 95) that seems joyously endless. Paragraph 22 (TP, 96) is a recapitulation: the poet, mildly successful (as with the "mild effects" of "The Skaters"), has realized the difference between two forms of happiness, if arbitrarily differentiated. He has remembered to forget; he has excluded the morbidity of a poisonous nostalgia. He has been truly a voice crying *in deserto* and has "died for the first time." Like Tolstoy's Levin after marriage, he is amazed that the world is still the same "ordinary daylight," and somehow this too seems miraculous (TP, 97).

For Ashbery, concluding "The System," silence itself is an answer, though discontinuity still reigns. Structural muteness is a positive idea and contributes to growth. In the empty spaces, absences, silences, discontinuities, and poetic pauses, something "as big as the universe" can grow (TP, 98). Thus, the poet of absence again redeems the *via negativa* of "this leaving-out business."

In paragraph 24 (TP, 99) the old man is now faced with a sudden imperative. Another voice, another persona, of unequalled Power, analyst or god or beloved, and all of these, speaks to the poet with solicitude: "the invisible bounty of my concern" (TP, 99).

The poet has arrived, and realizes in the antinomian sense that he has *always* been *in grace*. *New meaning* (TP, 99) is paradoxically recovered as a mislaid gift. Explicit sense is found in this reorientation: "this way of health" (TP, 99). The illumination of Ashbery's prose poem, his "breakthrough" in vulgarian terms, is a far cry from the collages of *The Tennis Court Oath*, which he admittedly put together in the most bleak period of his life.[13] Infantilism is identified in the self but is now partially controlled. "Imperious desire" is now partially mastered as in psychoanalytic terms by "ego" development and control (TP, 100). Merely glamorous dream imagery has given way to a less parodistic sense of mastery through humility and a surrender to the "invisible bounty" of the guiding voice. The image of a circle ("your wanderings have come full circle") in paragraph 26 (TP, 100) is employed to specify oneness, and moreover recovery and identification: "x equals y," as in "The New Spirit." Pluralism is involved in what for the poet seems an absurd regress into infinite detail and entangling instantaneities and minute particulars; so oneness is again invoked (TP, 101) but as no mad monism that would injure detail.

Film, both montage and consecutive, is rehearsed as a paradigm of this unified pluralism. But the celluloid vehicle is actually also paradigmatic of the poem, in which like a movie "the flame of a match can seem like an explosion on the sun" (TP, 103). The poem makes the familiar strange and also makes a "shapeless blur . . . meaningless as a carelessly exposed roll of film" (TP, 103) seem as shapely as a "real" story. The poet recalls what has been left out of this story, this meandering narration. Funnily animate, "the rejected chapters have taken over" (TP, 104). The poet imagines the future, accepts his uniqueness and his relativistic rightness in the history of literature: "At least we have that rightness that is rightfully ours" (TP, 105).

At last, the poet of "The System" can admit to his sad solipsistic pleasure: the film and poem as mirror. Autobiography, as in Wordsworth, as in Freud's self-analysis, is the necessary modality of Ashbery's darkened analysis. But the poet leaves the theatre of his own introspection and finds it difficult to readjust to the everyday's grey daylight. He wittily observes that it is like entering another kind of movie (TP, 106). This reminds one of the modulated labyrinths of "The Skaters." One never really takes off the final mask, or drops the final parodistic tone. The poet and lover are together, in another kind of *moving picture*, and the happy "allegory" announces its own end, though it does so by resuming the image of a "way" that develops open-endedly towards a cinematic, a "kinetic" future (TP, 106). The future is called "pragmatic" because the poet is now (not simply surrealistically) *using* it, as in "The academy of the future is/ Opening its doors" (RAM, 13). The poem ends, but reality too is a text. There is almost no end to the solipsistic decoding of signs; even the end is a sign.

At the end of "The System" the poet is in a position of mastery of the everyday and he will be able to master the future too. This mastery of the future has come by a kind of unsystematic system, and its mastery is one of the meanings of the "haphazard field of potentiality." Thus, "The System," despite some problems with its immense scale, despite its lack of song-like intrusions, ends with a convincing vision of having opened, for poet and reader, "this incommensurably wide way" (TP, 106).

Ashbery's poems can be usefully seen as complicated mosaics analogous to Islamic art; and the poem "The Recital" reminds us in its title of *The Koran*, which, as Ashbery has noted,[14] has been an influence. Arthur Arberry reminds us in the preface to his translation that the Koran's divisions (like those of Ashbery's poem and his usual work) are unequal quantities, called Suras.[15] As in Ashbery's manipulation of time, *The Koran* has no sequence comparable to the Old Testament. The Suras, as Arberry notes, have "embedded in them fragments received by Muhammad at widely differing dates" (p. 25) and in this sense *The Koran* is collagiste and anthological in somewhat the same way as Ashbery's composite and fragment-embedded work, while Ashbery's work too attempts to maintain something of the power of a sacred tome. The Suras, says Arberry, often have "incongruous parts" (p. 25), and Ashbery's work, we have noted again and again, accumulates by the most drastic anomalies of shape and scale.

The argument of "The Recital" is once again the problem of poetry itself, and the resolution of the negative, in a blank style of prose, along with the topic of finding a topic. Ashbery's poem begins with the colloquial and ironical dismissal of any perplexity: "All right. The problem is that there is no new problem" (TP, 107). The irony here is that this proposition remains the initiation for a whole field of poetic inquiry. The corollary of this paradox is carried forward in the parodistic tones of a bland, philosophically positivistic case in point: "It must awaken from the sleep of being part of some other, old problem, and by that time its new problematical existence will have already begun, carrying it forward into situations with which it cannot cope, . . ." (TP, 107). Ashbery raises the question of the pathos of probability, the pathos of freedom itself. The birds may sing beautifully in the dawn, and one is understandably charmed by discontinuity and the funny unexpectedness of it all, but isn't one also the more hurt by the fact that many permutations of this all-too-unpredictable world will be lost? This is a Beckett-like disillusion and seems to be a "poison" that the poet has drunk in his early lyric.

Of the many possibilities that the poet sees as possible, one is the route toward eternal gratification, of "polymorphous perversity," of infantile regression, perhaps, as in "The Skaters' " theme of childhood pleasures, and of desublimations, which the "waking" life of the poet is all too aware of as possibilities but which he senses can never be fulfilled. He sees the vagueness of his Utopian desires, and also the impossibility of these desires, and likens them to "children sulking because they cannot have the moon" (TP, 108). The poet visualizes this predicament as an unwillingness to deal with self-pity, and concludes that this is the cause for the *melancholia* that unreasonably overwhelms him. The poet then explicitly and didactically accuses himself of infantilism. This is a deposition of the Utopian, escapist, dream associations of his early poems. They lead not to gratification, but to the development of an enormous melancholy, which produces further inabilities, in colloquial terms, of "coping with reality,"—though it is difficult to locate this canonic cliché, Reality (unless you are a Realist).

Ashbery then follows with a paragraph that tries to examine the roots of "childishness." His analysis reads like a parody of cheap psychotherapeutic tracts, as in "we tried to patch things up," etc. (TP, 108). Childhood is seen as the tormenting time of jealousies and secrets, and development is seen as a development in revelation. The poet here names the earthly paradise he is desiring as a "down-to-earth Eden" (TP, 109). One is not sure whether this nonmalignant adult "situation" has ever been described adequately or convincingly by Ashbery. Perhaps "Blessing in Disguise" (RAM, 26), or the love alluded to in "Civilization and its Discontents" (RAM, 14) may be an adequate reminder of this topic of fulfilled love and "proper" perspective, though so many of the perspectives we have been examining are that of the "poison" and malignancy of improper perspectives and discontinuity.

The next paragraph announces the theme of devastation: "Fleeting and transient as the song of a bird" (TP, 109). The poetical task is seen as paradoxically and cruelly hopeless, because the very naming of joy becomes infinite, like the manner rejected in "The New Spirit" of *saying it all*. The poet, wrapped up in such naming, has exhausted his life with the poetical and becomes "a wistful parody" (TP, 109). Vitality is sapped by the effort of trying to revitalize memory for its Proustian resources. The true effort is one solely of the magician: "make them real, as if to live again were the only reality" (TP, 109). Probability itself begins to overwhelm the pulverized poet. Thus, the new manner, the aesthetic mode of expunging the *copula*, becomes necessary: "we must be selective" (TP, 109). But the pathos here is that the "tale" becomes a hermitage: "our private song, sung in the wilderness" (TP, 109).

The horror of the poet in a purgatorio of some mysterious making is resumed. "As leaves to a tree" was the naturalistic simile of John Keats when counselling on the production of poetry, an image of unforced Romantic bliss. Ashbery's Dantesque inversion, a true curse, is "the sorrow of continually doing something that you cannot name, of producing automatically as an apple tree produces apples this thing there is no name for" (TP, 110). The poet endures and advances stoically ("but your heart is pounding" [TP, 110]) in a life which has become numinous and penumbral. The poet has now seemingly lost the possibility of a content or skill, faced with a labyrinth that he himself extrudes, and that he is also powerless to escape.

The next paragraph ironically recapitulates the prelude: "All right. Then this new problem is the same one" (TP, 110). Ashbery then complains in the style of the French symbolists that the *ennui* he is facing is a veritable and objective phenomenon, and is "hydra-headed" (TP, 110). The poet offers in this didactic work another image of courage and endurance in the face of nonsensical, fantastic oppositions. The poet is to think of himself not as a feeble albatross, but as a sparrow that has forgotten his wings in battle with a cat (TP, 111). The poet must remember that no matter how limited his resources, the possibility is that the opposition is also not omnipotent. The true problem, Ashbery recognizes, is that the interiority of the opposition makes the battle all the more painful. Is the poet really counselling a struggle, or is he merely describing passively the possibility of a struggle? The description of courage is so cliché-ridden ("the vast plain of life" [TP, 111]) that it is hard to believe that the poet is not somehow already utterly doubting the possibility of a successful attack on the opposition. What he is doing is merely giving a skilful imitation of "correct" advice: a devastating tone.

Ashbery, in the following paragraph, makes a most explicit summation of his perplexity. After the despairing fragment, "It almost seens—," he discusses the horror of parody, when seen in a human context, that is, when the poet not only has begun to see the encrusted or degraded characteristic of styles and images, but of people themselves (TP, 111). This is comparable to the question of whether "The Waste Land" is merely, as Eliot once averred, the result of a grumble with personal life, or whether the manner of *symboliste* collage is an epochal situation in which the poet must "objectively" despair. At any rate, the prophecy of rottenness is heard and the heart-breaking conclusion is that "Appearances must be kept up at whatever cost until the Day of Judgment and afterward if possible" (TP, 112). The impulse is to maintain the facade, no matter how "wormy," and to let "no timbre ring false lest . . . its shame at last [become] real for all to see" (TP, 112). Ashbery mocks his own mask.

What follows is a reckoning of the possibility, aesthetically, of this horror, and curiously the poet shows once again an almost "utopian" sense, a grandiose confidence, in unfolding the possibilities. He describes his "all-but-terminated" work as having Grecian possibilities and "Romantic ardor minus the eccentricity" (TP, 112) but the reader cannot help wonder when the brutal self-laceration will intrude to knock down this perhaps hopeless estimation of the "chances" for success in a discontinuous world where Ashbery has given mortality and unsuccess the overwhelming odds. First Ashbery deposes the idea of an art without "artifice and artfulness" and acknowledges that the aesthetic is at least in congruence with "the rules," though he has never before made mention of any Boileau-like rules. But after discussing this capitulation to rules, and also to the desire for full-roundedness, Ashbery suddenly banishes the dream of complete gratification through art: "Perhaps no art, however gifted and well-intentioned, can supply what we were demanding of it" (TP, 113). The Rimbaldien demand for a self-sufficient art here meets with a sense of the probability of its failure. Art is modest and is aware of its limits.

The theme of misery, after this preceding paragraph on possibilities of success, is now able to intrude, and intrude with the viciousness of rhythmic intensity and minute particulars: "The days fly by; they do not cease" (TP, 113). The most heart-breaking image of minute and particulate "impression of absence" is summoned up in the line "the daylight had gone out of the day and it knew it" (TP, 113). This image reminds us of the mastery of the pathetic fallacy that Ashbery commands. The torpid and empty poet, understanding his lack of self-sufficiency and the uselessness of his most unconventional crutch, is still economic and "transparent."

Throughout "The Recital" Ashbery is able to make juxtapositions of clichés work a description of pitiless desolation. The clichés seem to remind us manneristically of the depression into which the poet has fallen: "The sky was still that nauseatingly cloying shade of blue" (TP, 114). Courage is now seen as "idiotic" and a matter of empty formulae. The *nonsensical* aspect is perhaps at its most insidious and extreme, with a lapse of coherency in the cold externals: "noticing too late that the landscape isn't making sense any more" (TP, 114). "Situational" ethics are deposed because no precepts can apply to situations which are always discontinuous, always new, and Ashbery is led to a final antinomian doubt: "there is even a doubt as to our own existence" (TP, 114). Ethics that are based on *agape* are rejected. Ashbery is led to suspect a final Dantesque curse: that the "beatitude" is taking place but that the poet is blind to it, though it is within (TP, 114).

An image of incoherence is presented in the illusion of a true bridge. Growth is said to be "from prudence to 'a timorous capacity,' in Wordsworth's phrase" (TP, 115) but unlike the Wordsworth of revitalized capacities, the poet is seen to be stuck on a Bridge of Sighs, which leads nowhere (TP, 115). The day ends in darkness, the tonic key is never reached, the perfect circle is broken. In imagery reminding one of Donne's anguish over the "new philosophy's doubts," Ashbery gives his figure of the new asymmetry: "the voyage always ends in a new key, although at the appointed place; a note has been added that destroys the whole fabric and the sense of the old as it was intended" (TP, 116). There is a sequence, but the sequence seems inconsequential, the tonality is paradoxically atonality.

Ethical dilemmas are posed most vividly toward the closure of any of Ashbery's work, and "The Recital" is the most direct of all these works. The poet asks directly whether he will be forced by his despair into a suicide or an incomprehensible affirmation. In another question, his former aesthetic of concealment, of fabulous rhetorical magic, is condemned: will there be another prolonged delay "disguised once again as an active life intelligently pursued?" (TP, 116).

The poet suddenly proceeds to a first-person intrusion: "As I thought about these things dusk began to invade my room" (TP, 116). The title of "The Recital" is ironically compared to "well-rehearsed lines" (TP, 116). Here the despair of Ecclesiastes is explicitly mocked: "Was there really nothing new under the sun?" (TP, 116). And the sensuous illusion of "well-rehearsed lines" themselves is seen as a possible answer to torpor.

Ashbery's inconclusion becomes a tangible object, and a possible answer in its tangible novelty, to the horror of the questions posed before. Poetry itself is again seen as the possibly haggard-seeming solution to the dilemma of the poet, though he is able to intrude a possibly damaging piece of criticism on its diction: "rearranged perhaps to give a wan impersonation of modernity and fecundity" (TP, 117). Ashbery's ending is indeed perhaps a "wan ending" like that alluded to in the detective story of "Rivers and Mountains" (p. 12). It is certainly a recital, as we have seen, of "well-rehearsed lines." The dilemma, though posed freshly, is resolved pretty much along Ashbery's usual principle: a rejection of principles, "idiotic formulae," a rejection of "the others," and an affirmation alone of the autistic playfulness of the process of *poesis* itself, seen as therapeutic confession becoming tangible novelty. The unassassinated poet has created himself.

"The Recital" is said to have "certain new elements," and the poem may indeed be seen to be *new* in its plain prose style, with no songlike interpolations, as in "The New Spirit," and also lacking the unbroken de Chirico-like streaming of clichés of "The System." Just as Joyce wanted *Ulysses* to be an "object," and "objecthood" among art objects is a fashionable theme of art critics in the '60s, so Ashbery contents himself with uncertainty on all points of reality except the novelty and satisfaction of the new poem, which he likens to a dawn. Ambiguity is also embraced: "the ambiguous situation one had come to know and even to tolerate, if not to love" (TP, 117). As the neurotic may be said to need his conflicts, so the poet has accepted his need of the "ambiguous." And what works most against any "definite break" is his tolerance of this habitual ambiguity.

Just as Eliot in *The Four Quartets* indulges in a somewhat self-praising attitude toward "the complete consort dancing together," so Ashbery ends with a note of poetic criticism, as so much of his work has tended to be: "The point was the synthesis of very simple elements" (TP, 117). One can't help wondering whether this conclusion is not slightly comparable to the scientistic analysis by Poe on his own technique or to Valery's claims and disclaimers concerning the consciousness of the artist. Suddenly Ashbery wonders why he wasn't able to make manifest this "simple" object before, this consolation of *poesis*. His answer is, like Eliot's, an affirmation of the need for propriety. Words must have a look of "worn familiarity" (TP, 117). He has rejected the glamor of his earlier style in favor of a drab inconspicuousness. The glamorous, aureate style is seen to "shatter" the intent of the poem, by causing "comment." Glamor leads to flamboyant dandyism, and just as the middle Shakespeare rejected the language of the merely golden, so Ashbery rejects his glamorous earlier style, in favor of a mixture of vocabularies, held in place by a fine prose. The collage itself begins then to fade, as the framing device of "The Recital" takes over as a final *repoussoir*.

The poet describes "a vast wetness" that signalizes the happy fusion and consolation of his last Adventure. There is now apathy concerning other final judgments, and a sense of self-esteem granted by the confession's success itself. The audience and the rewards of an audience are admitted: "There were new people watching and waiting" (TP, 118). The poet does not end with *agape*, the new people are not seen either as parodies or as neighbors, but as a bare audience, streaming out of a now empty hall. But the poet continues to affirm that the spectacle of *poesis* itself has been *cathartic, coherent,* and *lingering:* "the idea of the spectacle as something to be acted out and absorbed still hung in the air long after the last spectator had gone home to sleep" (TP, 118), and thus meaning has been rescued from meaninglessness, after all.

Conclusion

What induces one to reject a new poetry is often its complexity, its seeming opacity, or its central lack of old symmetries. As a matter of fact, as we have seen, Ashbery deliberately chose to abandon a derivative, early limpidity and purity of diction and structure for less melodious quantities: bleak collages, parodies, ironic prose pieces. The sense of beauty in Ashbery's work includes a sense of the degraded coherences, which must nevertheless be expunged.

Ashbery's defiant and humorous employment of a fertile formlessness as theme and style has been the main burden of his and our text. His poetry deals with the opacities of a context that seem to contrast only with silence. The darkness in Ashbery is rather clear, pointing to the breakdown of causality in contemporary thought and art. He has extended his insight into realms where being in the world seems unfamiliar and self-consuming and the linguistic content peculiarly disordered or hermetic. One of the central functions of an "abstract" poetry is to be aware of itself as non-discursive palpability. Such poetry is involved in particularity without a stable ground. That is the "meaning of meaninglessness," and Ashbery's poignant privacies affirm our elaborated sense of the certainty of uncertainty.

Biographical Note

John Ashbery was born in Rochester, N.Y., July 28, 1927, and grew up in Sodus, N.Y. He attended Deerfield Academy and Harvard (B.A., 1949), did graduate work at Columbia (M.A., 1951, thesis on Henry Green) and N.Y.U., specializing in French literature. He worked in publishing with Oxford University Press and McGraw-Hill, 1951–1955. He received a Fulbright to France (Montpellier) in 1955, renewed in 1956 for Paris, where he later became an art critic for the European Edition of the *New York Herald Tribune* and for *Art International* (Zurich), as well as Paris correspondent for *Art News* (New York).

Mr. Ashbery left Paris in 1965 and worked in New York as Executive Editor of *Art News* until 1972. He is currently a Professor of Writing at Brooklyn College and art editor of *New York* magazine. He has won many major awards for his poetry, including a Pulitzer Prize, a National Book Award, and a National Book Critics Circle Award for *Self-Portrait in a Convex Mirror* in 1975. His most recent works are *Three Plays, Houseboat Days,* and *A Vermont Notebook.*

I have purposely left the factual life here in a corner, as Josef

Albers said the signature left enough room for self-expression. I do not want to be like a hypothetical biographer of Stevens, a poet who did so much to delete the vulgar notion of biography from poetry. I agree, however, with Jakobson that a "vulgar anti-biographism" should not rule. I have tried to import my knowledge of Ashbery's temperament and character into all possible moments of my analysis. But a poem is not merely or primarily the consciousness of its author—it is a dynamism, a dissemination, a scattering of screens.

Notes

PROLEGOMENON. THE MIRROR STAGED

1. Arnold Hauser, *The Social History of Art*, Vol. 2 (New York: Random House, 1957–58), pp. 97–105.

CHAPTER 1. THE MEANING OF MEANINGLESSNESS

1. New York: E. P. Dutton, 1970, p. 30.

2. New York: Holt, Rinehart and Winston, 1966, p. 29.

3. The observations in this chapter are based substantially on interviews with John Ashbery, 1964–72. The chapter is printed with Mr. Ashbery's permission, and was first published in somewhat different form in *Field*, No. 5 (Fall 1971), pp. 32–45.

4. New Haven: Yale University Press, 1956.

5. New York: Viking, 1972, pp. 41–42.

6. Middletown, Conn.: Wesleyan University Press, 1957, p. 69.

7. New York: Tibor de Nagy, 1953, unpaged.

8. James Schuyler and John Ashbery, *A Nest of Ninnies* (New York: E. P. Dutton, 1969).

9. Giorgio de Chirico, *Hebdomeros* (New York: The Four Seasons Book Society, 1966).

10. *The Meaning of Meaning* (New York: Harcourt, Brace and World, 1923), pp. 186–87.

11. Ibid., 186.

CHAPTER 2. THE EARLY WORK

1. *An Artist's Theatre* (New York: Grove Press, 1960).
2. New York: New Directions, 1958.
3. Kenneth Koch, *Thank You and Other Poems* (New York: Grove Press, 1962), pp. 77–80.
4. Wallace Stevens, *Selected Poems* (New York: Random House, 1972), pp. 54 and 367.
5. John Ashbery, *The Poems* (New York: Tiber Press, 1960).

CHAPTER 3. THE PERIOD OF COLLAGE: *The Tennis Court Oath*

1. Interview with the author, November 1971.
2. The fact is that all the "rhymes" are short rhymes and a case might be made for the first stanza being a sort of ABAAAA pattern with the vowel and R sound in the last *accentual* beat in all lines but the second: *letter/mad/air/world/over me/Dwarf*. This carries into the second stanza's *daughter*, and echoes also internally in afternoon/her/centuries/utterly/daughter/employer. A full rhyme opens and closes the last line of the poem (May/Way) which also carries internally through the entire poem (*day/cake/late/played/always/late*). This is also lined up with a *cry/signed* series of internal rhymes.
3. Letter to author, Summer 1962.
4. *Selected Poems*, p. 83.

CHAPTER 4. THE POETRY OF PARODY: *Rivers and Mountains*

1. Interview with the author, November 1971.
2. Translated by James Strachey (New York: W. W. Norton, 1961).

CHAPTER 5. "THE SKATERS": AN ANALYSIS

1. "By Many Hands" (London: Sampson, Low, Marston, 1911).
2. Letter from Ashbery to the author, 1962.

3. Interview with the author, 1964.

4. Ibid., July 1972.

5. Frank O'Hara, *Collected Poems* (New York: Alfred A. Knopf, 1971), p. 266.

6. Ibid., p. 445.

7. Rainer Maria Rilke, *Duino Elegies*, trans. J. B. Leishman and Stephen Spender (New York: W. W. Norton, 1939), p. 71.

8. Interview with the author, 1971.

9. *The Meaning of Meaning*, pp. 186–87.

10. Ludwig Wittgenstein, *Tractatus Logico-Philosophicus*, trans. D. Pears (London: Routledge and Kegan Paul, 1961).

CHAPTER 6. MEDITATIONS ON PROBABILITY: *Three Poems*

1. Ashbery, conversation with author, reported in *Field*, No. 5 (Fall 1971), p. 35.

2. Ashbery, interview with author, November 1971.

3. Ibid., 1971.

4. Kenneth Rexroth, comment on *Rivers and Mountains* (New York: Holt, 1966), book jacket.

5. Interview with the author, 1964, New York.

6. Rilke, *Selected Works*, trans. J. B. Leishman (New York: New Directions, 1960), p. 146.

7. Frank O'Hara, *Collected Works* (New York: Alfred Knopf, 1971).

8. Interview with Ashbery, 1971.

9. Ibid., 1971.

10. John Ashbery, *The Double Dream of Spring* (New York: E. P. Dutton, 1970), p. 78.

11. Interview with author, October 1972.

12. John Ashbery with Kenneth Koch, *A Conversation* (Arizona: Interview Press, undated).

13. Interview with author, November 1971.

14. Ibid.

15. *The Koran Interpreted*, ed. and trans. Arthur Arberry (New York: Macmillan, 1955), pp. 25–28.

Selected Bibliography

Turandot and Other Poems. New York: Tibor de Nagy, 1953.

Some Trees. New Haven: Yale University Press, 1956 (repr. New York: Ecco Press, 1978).

The Poems. New York: Tiber Press, 1960.

The Tennis Court Oath. Middletown, Conn.: Wesleyan University Press, 1962.

Rivers and Mountains. New York: Holt, Rinehart and Winston, 1967 (repr. New York: Ecco Press, 1977).

Selected Poems. London: Jonathan Cape Ltd., 1967.

A Nest of Ninnies (with James Schuyler). New York: E. P. Dutton, 1969 (repr. Calais, Vt.: Z Press, 1975).

The Double Dream of Spring. New York: E. P. Dutton, 1970 (repr. New York: Ecco Press, 1976).

Three Poems. New York: Viking Press, 1972

The Vermont Notebook. Los Angeles: Black Sparrow Press, 1975.

Self-Portrait in a Convex Mirror. New York: Viking Press, 1975.

Houseboat Days. New York: Viking Press, 1977.

Three Plays. Calais, Vermont: Z Press, 1978.

NOTE: The student is advised to consult David K. Kermani, *John Ashbery: A Comprehensive Bibliography* (New York and London: Garland Publishing Inc., 1976) for its fine listing of Ashbery's art criticism, translations, editions, catalogues, and miscellanea.

Index